Intimate Conversations

with the

HOLY SPIRIT

Matthew Robert Payne

Table of Contents

Introduction

When the video series was started that I have made this book from, it was simply my intention to get to know the Holy Spirit and bless the regular viewers of my videos. I have a series of Conversations with God, and I simply wanted to capture a record of my new conversations with the Holy Spirit. It wasn't till a few videos in that I even thought to make a book from them, and it wasn't till later that I began to switch my attention to the reader and not just myself. Initially the conversations were about me and my issues in life.

I hope that you can bear this in mind during the early questions and subjects in this book. This is a look at my personal life and my interactions with the Holy Spirit first and foremost, and then in later questions it was turned, hopefully, to a wider audience. I am a fallen man, and a sinner, and someone who is very transparent when it comes to my struggles with sin. I hope as my sin-life is mentioned that you can see that this book is about one man's journey in life, and casts a view of the personality of the Holy Spirit in all matters.

I don't profess to be as popular as Benny Hinn and his book "*Good Morning, Holy Spirit*" or Madam Jeanne Guyon and her intimacy with God, but I am a simple writer with a deep faith, and a person that is not perfect by any means. I pray that this book really touches you.

[Conversations with the Holy Spirit: Part 1]

I've been having conversations with the Holy Spirit of late, and it's the middle of the night now, and I just woke up. I've just listened to a YouTube video that was interesting, and I feel that the Holy Spirit wants to have a conversation with me now and have it recorded. I've had conversations with Jesus, and I have had conversations with the Father that ended up in videos and books. I haven't had conversations with the Holy Spirit before, I don't think. I will proceed simply to ask the Holy Spirit questions and see what he answers.

Question 1: First of all, what do you think of this Coronavirus and the shutdown of the church?

Conversation recorded April 2, 2020

Holy Spirit says: People are amazed straightaway with how the authorities who run the world are able to shut down the church. You've been saying for a long time that people need to obey Jesus. People need to be able to hear from Jesus. People need to be able to hear from the Holy Spirit. You have been telling people that it's important, and for many people in your audience that was falling on deaf ears.

I suppose that people probably just can't comprehend the fact that the church, whether it be church buildings, church fellowship, or church gatherings, could be shut down. People look at China, North Korea and Russia, and see that in those countries having Church and meeting and fellowshipping may be difficult. That's okay for those countries, you say, because of bad governments who are communist and socialist, but you think that would never happen in the West.

We're a free nation under God, and we fellowship with God, and that's part of the constitution. It would never happen; but here it is, here it is now. Here in Australia it is illegal to have a meeting with more than two people. So here it is in a few short weeks - the church has been shut down. It is such a surprise to many people. Everything happens for a reason.

There is a time of transition happening in the Bride of Christ; the bride has to become a bride and become faithful and become needful, and become emotionally and spiritually and passionately attached to the Savior. For many people, church was just an event or a religion, or just part of their life. We got to transition out of that into a person's faith being the most important thing in their life.

There are multiple reasons for different things that are happening right now, and it can't be just answered in one answer, but there are multiple things happening. God wants to restore his relationship with mankind, and he needs to maintain trying to act via faith, rather than through religion and through set rules and through circumstances. We want to communicate with people face-to-face, word-for-word. We want people to know us and speak to us and fellowship with us, instead of going through the routine of religion and through a set smokescreen, a set routine that people have.

We've got the warning in Revelation 18 to "come out of her", and some people, the brightest people, have come out of her and are giving their best. Some people with good hearts came out of the institution and didn't go back or didn't feel guilty.

There is part of the church, the remnant, the bridal church, who walk in freedom, but then there are people who needed religion, who needed that structure, that still stayed behind. Therefore, it was needful for us to pull everyone out of church for people to consider: to consider what's happening and consider their future. I hope that you enjoyed this conversation.

[Conversations with the Holy Spirit: Part 2]

Hi, this is Matthew Robert Payne, Today, I'm going to talk to the Holy Spirit for a little chat. Today, we're going to talk and to start with unforgiveness.

Question 2: Holy Spirit, how do you deal with people who you haven't forgiven?

Conversation recorded on April 3, 2020

Matthew has had some hurts in his life that hurt so much he couldn't immediately forgive. You know one time his mother rang him up and got him admitted to a psych ward, and he had a hard time forgiving his mother. Just recently in August 2019, his mother died, and his sister and his father decided that Matthew couldn't come to the funeral. Matthew didn't get invited to the funeral - that really hurt him, and it just resulted in unforgiveness towards his sister.

Jesus warns in the Gospels in Matthew, that if you don't forgive, you won't be forgiven either. That verse can tend to help some people try and forgive too early. While it looks like you have some emotion around forgiveness, you may try and forgive; but if you don't do a proper job, it'll just settle down in your spirit as bitterness. And bitterness can cause all sorts of sicknesses, and all sorts of problems and blockages in the flow of the Holy Ghost in your life. So, we suggested to Matthew that you bring the people up in prayer and you just say to the Father, "Father, give me the grace to forgive this person some time."

You simply say, "I want to forgive them, but I haven't got the grace to forgive them right now. So please, I pray that you give me the grace to forgive in the future." And when you've processed emotions and when you've come through life in a substantial way, then you get to the stage where you can forgive. And for Matthew, for his younger brother and his sister, it was hard to forgive them the other day.

So Holy Spirit, how do you deal with people who you haven't forgiven?

I suppose unforgiveness can destroy friendships, and some people might just treat the people like nothing happened. And you can do that and not be changing your personality - that would be it. But it's quite alright for two people to coexist in a workplace or something, knowing that they don't like each other, knowing that there's a sort of feud. If you tell the person quite plainly, "I can't forgive you at the moment, and I'm not going to pretend that I have, so can you keep your distance?"

That would be quite an alright thing to say to a person if you had to work in a workplace with them. They often will respect that more than you pretending nothing happened.

Question 3: Have you got any other tips for the workplace?

Well, Matthew has shared this another time. If this was in the workplace or this was in life, you can have a person who really didn't like you constantly having arguments. You can buy them a set of ten cinemas tickets and say to the person, "I know we got into it yesterday, and what was said back and forth wasn't very nice. I hope you like the cinema, as here are some free tickets. You know, probably it's my fault what's been happening, because I normally get on well with people - and with you, I don't seem to. So probably it's my fault. I hope you enjoy the cinema. When you are in the cinema, just remember that I bought this for you, and I hope that things can be better in our relationship in the future. God bless you."

That is an example of blessing your enemies, and the Bible says bless your enemies and feed guys who are against you or give them a drink. People misunderstand those verses; they don't have a modern application for them. If you had a fall-out with a woman, for instance at work, and you're another woman or a man, you could buy some flowers and give them to her. Just be creative - blessing your enemies isn't just saying "God bless you," it's actually doing something that blesses them.

Question 4: Have you got suggestions for growing more intimate with Jesus?

The more you know about Jesus, the more intimate you can become with him. Matthew has a few books that will help you with this. You can source out these three books: *Jesus Speaks Today, Finding Intimacy with Jesus Made Simple.* and *7 Keys to Intimacy with Jesus.* These books would be very helpful for you.

Socially speaking, Jesus is just like anyone. The more time you spend with him, the more questions you ask him, the greater you know him.

You know, when you're with a friend, you listen to them and ask some questions, and ask some questions about their answers, and ask some questions about their answers to the questions that you ask about their answers. You just continue questioning and asking and discussing things.

Getting to know Jesus is no different. Jesus is just words on the page in the Bible and this may not allow you to know Jesus really well. But if you develop a relationship where you can see him and talk to him, or you can develop relationship where you can talk to him back and forth, you will develop a lot deeper relationship. First of all, you need to learn how to speak back and forth with him. You may find this book helpful in that regard: *How to Hear God's Voice.*

You can ask him questions and asking him questions will grow your relationship in a better way than just knowing him by books, sermons and attending a church. You have an instance now with Coronavirus where we're not going to church right at the moment. It's a good time to get to know us in the Trinity, and I am part of the Trinity. When you talk to Jesus, essentially, it's my voice that brings Jesus to you, and it's much communication that brings the Father's voice to you. And each of our voices have a different resonance; they have a different frequency.

When you're used to speaking to us, you can tell which one of us it is, and Matthew can tell when it's any of us. Jesus is really worth getting to know, and I'm worth getting to know. These videos that the book is going to come from are the way that Matthew can get to know me in a better way, as well as the audience. It's very interesting speaking to you. There are not many books devoted to me, and there probably wouldn't be many books where I'm speaking. I sound a little bit like Matthew because so much of what Matthew says is inspired by me. I enjoy speaking, so I hope that you enjoyed this video.

[Conversations with the Holy Spirit: Part 3]

Question 5: What do you love about me?

Conversation recorded on April 4, 2020

I love a number of things; I can't tell how long you want me to talk. I love your tenacity, which to people who don't know tenacity means I love your ability to get up and keep on going. This is song that the band The Mighty Bosstones sang: "I get knocked down, but I get up again. No one's ever going to keep me down. I get knocked down, but I get up again." That's just the story of your life. You keep on getting knocked down, but you keep getting up. I also love your obedience. You can be told to do things by me or Jesus, or even the anti-Christ spirits who masquerade as Jesus, and you do them. One of my favorite things was when you stripped off naked and did five dive-bombs in a stranger's pool. This was an anti-Christ spirit that pretended to be Jesus to you that told you to do it, but you did it. He told you if you do five naked dive bombs that that he would arrange to house all the homeless in Sydney. You were very messed up mentally when you heard that, but your love for the homeless compelled you to obey and you stripped off and did the five dive bombs.

The people of heaven just watch the film of those dive bombs and they crack up. Anytime heaven wants to laugh, all of heaven will play that and have a good laugh. That act was just crazy obedient. For many years, you've known that I'm one of Trinity that you obey, and you've done a lot of things we have asked you to.

For many years you have been obeying as a type of insurance on your life. It's like you've been insuring yourself to make sure that you go to heaven. You've been buying good works insurance. But we have told you recently that anything that comes which is directed by the Holy Spirit isn't striving, that's actually walking in the will of God.

So, you have gone from just striving and doing godly things like writing articles, to actually obeying Jesus and me and moving in the Holy Spirit and walking in the Holy Spirit. To be honest, I just so enjoy your obedience. And if you're listening, obedience has a number of levels. You can find out the fifty commands of Jesus in an article that Matthew has written on Google, and you can find it on Google if you search *"The Fifty Commandments of Jesus."* You can start to follow them, and that's obedience.

But another form of obedience, once you learn to hear my voice, is then I can tell you to do a whole lot of other things which you need to make a conscious effort to obey.

Here is an example. Matthew had $740 in his PayPal account, and he was led by my Spirit to give two hundred to one of his friends today. We told him early on in the conversation to give the money to his friend, but Matthew was not wanting to give two hundred Australian dollars to his friend. We worked on him by repeating it, and then twenty minutes into the conversation he asked his friend did they need 150 US dollars for something (which is 200 Australian dollars) They said yes, there was a bill that they needed to pay that was outstanding, and that they were worried about. So, Matthew transferred the money before they got off the phone.

The way that you obey me is astounding. You can be sure if we ask you to do anything, we will also give you the grace to do what we ask of you. Any spirit asking you to do that does not supply you the grace to do it, is not a Spirit of God.

We take you to another level of obedience. When you're going out to get coffee or when you're going out, you can be told to go and approach and tell a person this or go and see that person and tell them this. Or to a guy, collecting money on the street for the homeless, we can tell you to go to the bank and get twenty dollars and give it to him. That's just another level of obedience. Matthew, you are crazy obedient. We will send you many miles away just to speak to one person.

And we know that we can send you anywhere. We know that we can organize your life for you to bless anyone. It's just a blessing for us, and the more scripture that you have in you, if you have a prophetic gift, if you have one of the gifts of the Holy Spirit, it can really be used in this life. I really appreciate people who learn to obey. And it's all out of love, like Jesus said in John 15 - no greater love has a man than laying down his life for his friend, laying down his life for a brother.

When you lay down your life for another, that is what approaching people and sharing the gospel with them really is. Approaching people and encouraging them is way of showing the love of God to people. This laying down your life is laying down your pride, laying down your will, and doing the will of the Holy Spirit and doing our will. You will find that Matthew is very dangerous when he goes out. He flies behind enemy lines; he goes and takes ground in people's lives, and he's dangerous.

I really enjoy his honesty, how honest and transparent he is. I really enjoy how honest and transparent Mathew is. You are just amazingly equipped. You took a passage out of a book that said that the *law of candor* means that if you say disparaging or bad comments about your life, people will believe you when you're making out the point. If you admit bad things about your life people will believe you more, because you've been so transparent about how bad you've been. In your book and videos, you have taken the *law of candor* to another level. Michael Van Vlymen, your friend and a popular Christian author, in one of his conversations with you said that he's just amazed at how often you'll throw yourself under a bus to make a simple point.

And he's just amazed, and we're amazed, and heaven is amazed every day by you. I want you to know that every day you go out on the bus to get shopping, we get excited. Every time you're up, we're excited. Heaven loves to come for a walk down to the gas station to get things in the middle of the night and your interactions with the gas station staff. Heaven loves to see you. No matter what the stage or whatever state you're in, heaven enjoys you.

[Conversations with the Holy Spirit: Part 4]

Question 6: What have you to say about religion and the right way?

Conversation recorded on April 4, 2020

One of the chief things that Jesus wanted his followers to do was to shine. One of the chief things that Jesus Christ wanted people to do is to emulate him. John in 1 John 2:3-6 says those who abide must walk like he does.

"[3] Now by this we know that we know Him, if we keep His commandments. [4] He who says, "I know Him," and does not keep His commandments, is a liar, and the truth is not in him. [5] But whoever keeps His word, truly the love of God is perfected in him. By this we know that we are in Him. [6] He who says he abides in Him ought himself also to walk just as He walked."

John was talking about Jesus. John was saying if you say you're close to Jesus, then you should be acting like Jesus. The Apostle Paul said, in 1 Corinthians 11:1, "Imitate me as I imitate Christ."

Too often, I hear the Christian message being taught about being religious, about going to church, about singing songs, about tithing, and about doing the things religious people do. Well, Buddhists have a temple that they go to, and Buddhists pray, and Buddhists give offerings. Muslims go to a mosque, Muslims bow the knee, and Muslims prays. The people of other gods need to meet representations of Jesus Christ, and Matthew's found that it's helpful to always to have a friend that demonstrates a manifestation of Jesus to him.

You don't just need Jesus in heaven to talk to; you need someone that manifests Jesus on earth for you to connect with to have a good connection with Jesus.

Matthew speaks:

I have found that myself from time to time, Holy Spirit, I find that I do need that connection to Jesus; I do need someone to manifest Jesus sometimes for me to have a proper connection to Jesus himself. You were saying that the Christian Church preaches religion, and it does; it teaches religion.

I find it rare for them to say that you can be like Jesus, that you can act like Jesus, that you can be a demonstration of Jesus. But Jesus said it quite clearly that we shouldn't hide our light; we should shine a light brightly. And these are times that remind me of Isaiah 60:

"Arise, shine;
For your light has come!
And the glory of the Lord is risen upon you.
2 For behold, the darkness shall cover the earth,
And deep darkness the people;
But the Lord will arise over you,
And His glory will be seen upon you.
3 The Gentiles shall come to your light,
And kings to the brightness of your rising."

We should be living that right now, that should be what we're doing, that should be how we're living these days.

Holy Spirit says:

It is the desire of Jesus for people to shine. Jesus said it clearly in Matthew 5:14-16:

[14] "You are the light of the world. A city that is set on a hill cannot be hidden. [15] Nor do they light a lamp and put it under a basket, but on a lampstand, and it gives light to all *who are* in the house. [16] Let your light so shine before men, that they may see your good works and glorify your Father in heaven."

It's the desire of Jesus for people to walk in communion with me and fellowship with me and obey what I say. The daily commands and the commands that you hear each day from me, and the directions you get each day from me, are what I want you to follow.

Jesus says in John 15:4-5: "[4] Abide in Me, and I in you. As the branch cannot bear fruit of itself, unless it abides in the vine, neither can you, unless you abide in Me. [5] "I am the vine, you *are* the branches. He who abides in Me, and I in him, bears much fruit; for without Me you can do nothing."

Every person should be able to be led by me; every person who is a Christian should be able to hear me and should be able to be led by me. And their lifestyle should be one that demonstrates the love and the compassion and the kindness and the goodness of Jesus Christ. Kindness and goodness and compassion I just mentioned as fruits of the spirit - compassion isn't mentioned, but it is an outwork of love, which is mentioned. But true to the Spirit is what people should partake of you, they should come to you and get kindness, they should come to you and get goodness. They should come to you and get joy and love and peace. A Christian life should be a demonstration of grace, it should be a demonstration of the life of Jesus.

A Christian should be full of joy, full of love, goodness, kindness, and that should be the fruit that people partake. The Bible says in Psalm 1:3:

"He shall be like a tree
Planted by the rivers of water,

That brings forth its fruit in its season,
Whose leaf also shall not wither;
And whatever he does shall prosper."

You should be that fruitful tree; you should be that demonstration of the grace of God. You should be the demonstration of the love of God. Jesus didn't come and die just to save people's sins. Jesus came so that you could be a duplicate, that he would be the firstborn of the resurrection. And he'd have many sons that would follow him and act like him and behave like him. And it's a special calling I have on you, and the listeners of the series. You want to learn how to walk like Jesus; you want to learn how to be like Jesus. You want to be not of this world. This is a special time where you can act differently; you can act without fear. You can act and shine a beam of light; you should shine with Jesus' light.

So much religion doesn't teach that you can be like Jesus, and yet that was the purpose of him coming - to demonstrate who you're meant to be like, and they can't. There are people that live properly and shine Jesus in the right way. There are people like Todd White, who have travelled the world; and when someone needs healing, he heals, and when someone needs money, he gives them money. And it shouldn't just be one person; it shouldn't just be one person. Out of thousands of people, it should be all of you. You should all be sons of God.

[Conversations with the Holy Spirit: Part 5]

Question 7: What are the reasons you allowed my computer to break?

Conversation recorded on April 9, 2020

Matthew, we have a reason behind everything that we do. One of the major reasons of taking the computer out of action is taking you out of action; you used to spend a lot of time on the computer, on Facebook.

When we take your computer away from you, it gives us a lot more time back in, it gives us more time with you. From that understanding, your computer may not fix itself up - you may have to save for a new one. But all things work together for good. This gives us an opportunity to speak to you in intimacy and develop intimacy with you. It gives us more time with you as you are spending so much time on the computer and diverting your time to doing other things. It gives us more time to actually speak to you.

If you are a reader here, you might have habits; you may have time that you spend on the Internet, time that you spend watching TV. You may have special things that you spend time with. Sometimes it takes a sacrifice to sacrifice something to spend time with us and develop intimacy. Every good thing done in Christian works comes out of intimacy, and obviously it's like the engine room to everything great in Christian circles. Of course, prayer is important, but prayer is part of intimacy.

Prayer is one portion of being intimate with your God. When you're intimate with your God, you're speaking to your God, and God is speaking back to you.

Matthew, you read in a personal prophecy that God was going to change the way you did things and change his methods, and you're going to come across change. You understand that, as you read that in the prophecy, you just received that things are going to change - the prophecy changes your perspective. And that's what we wanted you to do with what we asked for. We just need you rest for a while and not be so busy. Wetting your computer has caused you to go into this stage of not being on the computer all day.

It's just changed your whole lifestyle, which is a good thing for us and gives us more time when we're with you. You've got written there that you had spent some time with your mother today, and you spent some time talking to her, and she was pleased to see you; she's pleased to talk to you from heaven. She was pleased to direct you and direct you to different things, and show you different things, and so she enjoys her life now in heaven and having the ability to visit you each day. She loves being here for you, and we've been working on you in the last three weeks on the subject of forgiveness.

We have been showing you people that you haven't forgiven, and you're working on your heart to posture yourself to forgive those people. The more you shine, the more you stand out, the more people come up against you, and the more people strike out at you, and that's not a good thing. But that's what happens. And so, you constantly have to be vigilant in the cycle of forgiveness.

Unforgiveness muddies the waters. A good example would be water in the stream being muddied up by people, having people playing in the mud and stirring it up, and it's not until the sediment comes out of the water that the water isn't muddied up. Your life can be muddied up by the water with unforgiveness in it. It's not a pure water till you forgive. I enjoy watching you; I enjoy being part of your life, and I enjoy doing these short videos for you and sharing with you. I am happy that people are watching, and happy also watching these things happen.

Update by Matthew

Written on 1st of July 2020

It is months later now. I spend a lot less time on Facebook now and I have entered into a time of rest. There is more communication with the Trinity, there is more relaxation and there is more communication with saints and angels. I have begun to live a life without striving and it seems the loss of my computer for a time sparked this change and it has not reverted back. There are good reasons for bad things happening.

[Conversations with the Holy Spirit: Part 6]

Subject 8: Holy Spirit speaks on a perfect God, finances, bipolar, attacks, being Jesus, His future.

Conversation recorded on April 12th, 2020

Today, I am wearing one of my T-shirts: "Everything God does is perfect."

Holy Spirit

You know, Matthew, that everything God does is perfect, and people look at the Old Testament and they judge God; people look at their life, and the things going wrong, and they judge God. People look at unanswered prayers, and heartache in their lives, and struggles in their life, and they blame God.

And so, this T-shirt you are wearing, it's a very confrontational shirt to wear, even though everything God does is perfect. Most people don't agree with that; they don't agree, and their lives are hard, their lives are tough. It seems many things in their life aren't fair, and they blame those things on God many times, and that can be hard.

The first subject we got here is finances, and your computer went wrong, and you're starting to try and save money to get a new computer.

It may surprise people, but the kingdom doesn't so much work very often with excess, unless you know where to put the excess. For once, Matthew had an excess of money and was able to use it on his new computer. But most ministries don't operate on excess, though good ones can.

For instance, Matthew knows of a very popular ministry by a woman where eighty percent of her ministry's income is given to other ministries by her. Her ministry runs on excess. Matthew has met an international prophet who has seventy-five percent of his income that comes in through his ministry that he gives to other ministries.

Matthew's ministry is not at that point yet where he's got an overflow like that. But we use everything; we use his intellect, we use his income, we use his theology. We use his innocence, his gullibility, the fact that he's gullible. We use his mental illness; we use his many thoughts; we use everything. We do that to demonstrate that anyone can be used by God.

Matthew is influencing the people that God uses, that we use to teach people. He's a tremendous teacher with a lot of wisdom. That is like a message for you people. If Matthew being a diabetic, overweight, mentally ill and self-taught with no Bible College education can minister to thousands, so can you. If Mathew can impress people, so can you. I hope as you watch this, or possibly read this in the future, I hope that you realize that even your deficits can become positives.

Mathew's bipolar allows him to stay up for two or three nights; he can get high or elevated or anointed, whatever word you want to use. He can speak for 12 hours straight. We can use that mental illness for the positive; when not many people can do that. The Apostle Paul spoke for 18 hours in one session, from midday to 6 am the next morning. You know that time because, on the twelfth hour, someone fell out of the roof and died - and Paul raised him from the dead.

Matthew is in this reverse sleep pattern that he's staying up most of the night now and sleeping most of the day. Years ago, he had a four-year sleep sickness in which he used to sleep about 18 hours a day. At the moment it's like the enemy is trying to stifle him back into that and he's just not going to receive it, he's just not going to have it. The sleep sickness was very debilitating. So, we're going to have him go out today. When he goes out, he's a weapon, we really use him; he is what we call weaponized.

I will direct you to when you see films of men attaching bombs to aircraft, fighter jets. When they've attached all the bombs and missiles to them, then they're fully weaponized. Matthew just has to put on one of his T-shirts and be in a good mood, and he's weaponized. When he is in a good mood and feeling evangelistic, he becomes a real weapon. He goes out and does damage to Satan's Kingdom. We've got him up tonight, and we'll keep him busy tonight - and hopefully in the daytime, when it's time to go out, he'll be able to go and make an impact on a few people. We have told him that he is not to worry about the sleep pattern. Matthew will handle it. Like everything you've done in the last 20 years, you've coped, and you'll cope again.

Matthew's update: July 1ˢᵗ, 2020

The sleep pattern settled down and I got in control and back to normal sleep patterns. This was a real worry for me as the four years I suffered from sleeping 18 hours a day was very depression- filled. The Holy Spirit was right when he said I would handle it.

Holy Spirit:

The next subject you want to talk about is the attacks.

This is Matthew:

Yes, I've been getting attacked by witches that drove me to a psychiatric ward less and less. I usually get attacked every time I get up to go to the toilet when I'm watching TV, in my breaks. I get attacked, and this woman witch attacks me. The reason I get attacked in advertisement breaks is that it is the only time my mind is not engaged with the TV. The witch gets quite surprised, however, that I can cut her voice off halfway through her insults.

The witchcraft attacks are diminishing, and I want to thank you, Holy Spirit, for doing a work to get me into a psych ward and letting them give me medication to help me cope a whole lot better.

Holy Spirit:

Matthew, I want you to know that everything God does is perfect, like your T-shirt says. You were cycling from one delusion to the next, and you were just quite delusional up until we put you in the hospital. We put you in the hospital when they up your dosage of medication, and that's for a reason. Some people can talk of healing, and some people have a healing gift. Some people are happy with medication, and we're happy for you to be on this medication, and for you not to be psychotic. People who have been watching Matthew for last year may have noticed some of his psychosis in some of his videos. They would be happy he is well now.

We have asked Matthew to keep all his videos up online so people can see what mental illness looks like. You can see what psychosis is; you can see what mental illness is. It's plain to see what a common person can go through. He's quite able to see how he's deceived there; he's deluded there. A funny thing people might not know about delusion is when you're in a delusion, you don't know that you are in it. You can suspect you might be not right, but when you're deluded, you're fully deluded.

That's why when in the body of Christ, one member calls out another member, and humbly shares that the other member is deceived, and the person receives it that they are deluded, it can be so helpful. Sometimes to get the person out of the delusion, as a friend, you may have to speak up.

I want you to know, Matthew and other people, that your episodes where you have flowed in your bipolar suit us. No matter what attacks you, it is true that no weapon formed against you shall prosper. You are precious to us, and to the people that are listening to these messages and reading eventually, if it's ever going to become a book - you're precious to God. No matter how many spiritual attacks or mental or physical, biological, or any sort of attack comes against you, you will prosper. No matter what attack comes at you, you are still special. It's all still special to me, still special to Jesus; it's special to the Father.

Matthew:

So, I can understand you saying that you said that to the Holy Spirit, which is pretty amazing.

Holy Spirit:

This is a theme that's coming up in Matthew's teaching more and more often. People need a physical Jesus to hold on to, people need a real person manifesting the presence and the spirit of Jesus, and people need that. People just can't have this God in the sky; people need a God in the flesh. Just like Jesus is in the flesh, you need to be Jesus in the flesh for someone.

The more people that you've got in your life that Jesus in the flesh, the more you can understand the Jesus in heaven. Matthew teaches that, and he's quite firm on the teaching that we really need to demonstrate Jesus; we really need to obey Jesus. As people on earth, you really need to obey Jesus. That's what we need you to do; we need you to obey Jesus. We don't need you to be religious; we don't need you saving people and leading people to Christ; we need you to be Christ.

God should not be talked about; he should be experienced. You shouldn't just talk about your experiences with God; you should let people have an experience of God when they meet you.

People shouldn't have to wait to get to heaven to meet God; they should meet God in you. The difference between you and God is nothing; you can be an incarnate Jesus on earth.

We want you to grow closer and closer to Jesus so that you can be him, so you can be like him, so you can be his representative on earth.

He wants you to be his ambassador. An ambassador represents a country in another country. You should be so much of the kingdom of heaven that when you're on earth, you're an ambassador from the kingdom of heaven. That's not found in wealth and riches, and luxury and big names, and big titles, it's found in humility and service and love. I know there are many people teaching that the more money you have, the more riches you have, the more successful you are, the more God has blessed you. This can be true in some respects, but only if the wealth is being used to prosper the kingdom and not just an individual's life. There are some people that preach that you got to be poor, too. God can use poor people powerfully also. You should use your money to make it a better world.

Of course, you need clothes, of course you need a top, you need some pants, you need a skirt. You need a dress; you need shoes. Of course, the world has needs, but you don't have to have the best luxury brands and everything. I need you all to grow closer to the Holy Spirit, to me, and through Jesus and the Father; we need you to grow in love and compassion for the world.

Jesus said if you want to follow me, you must deny yourself, pick up your cross and follow me. And Matthew has got a whole book about that subject. That book is called *"Do We Do What Jesus Said?"* So, we need you to grow closer, we need you to deny yourself, deny yourself time. We need you to do other things and devote time to get to know God.

This is Matthew:

It's clear that you understand my future, Holy Spirit. Can you speak about that?

Holy Spirit:

Matthew, you go through times of worry and concern, and sleeping all day, and not being able to sleep at night, and that concerns you. You're worried; it's hard for you. Sometimes you get worried about who you are and what you are and what is your real future. But it's important for you to know your future. We've got your future all planned out, and you've got a good future. You will come to a place where you are not so worried about your future, and you will not be striving but just content for us to let it play out naturally.

But it does take time, and you got to lay down your life. But we've got a good process of germination, growing, dying, germination, growing, dying. There's this process that we take you on, and you've just got to trust our process.

Update by Matthew on July 1st, 2020:

Through a hospital admission to a psychiatric ward and an adjustment to my medication, and another hospital admission for Diabetes and some great conversations with the Holy Spirit and the Trinity, I have come to a good place of rest. I found I am content and happy with my life and I don't seem to be striving as much. As I go through this to correct the typing and edit this, I can see that the Holy Spirit was right that everything was going to work out fine.

[Conversations with the Holy Spirit: Part 7]

Question 8: How do I deal with my stress?

Conversation recorded on April 21, 2020

Matthew:

I had been having really bad internet problems as a result of not having enough download capacity, and the internet slowed for me and I had to change my plan. I also had a Visa whose expiry date came due and so it was out of date, and so I had to change the card with my internet firm for billing, but I could not log on or contact them by phone. They had very limited people answering phones due to the Coronavirus outbreak - and so I was stressing my internet would be cut off for not paying my bill. I tend to really stress about things. I had this conversation in the middle of this situation or just after I had it.

Holy Spirit says:

It's a special time for Matthew, and it's good for me to be getting on and speaking to you all. We told you, I told you, your mother told you, we try to reassure you that your problems would get fixed. But the thing with you people on the earth is that you worry about things. It's like a specific track in your mind just to worry. You've heard before, and you've quoted it to other people, *"don't worry, pray,"* Matthew. But you prefer to worry instead of praying. We told you it would be okay and you didn't believe us. I want that to be an example to everyone listening, that everything God does is perfect. Sometimes we should remember the Scriptures, remember the promises of the Bible over our situation.

There are Bible verses that say you can conquer problems; there are Bible verses that say that everything will be okay, Matthew. Yet you are still stressed, and still worried about that. The internet really slowed down a couple of days ago, and you were having a hard time uploading videos. It took two and a half hours to upload a ten-minute video because the internet company had slowed your speed. And normally, a 10-minute video takes 20minutes to upload, and so that was stressing you.

You let a whole lot of things stress you, and people are listening or reading in the future; it's important that you either trust God or you don't trust God. If you put your trust in God, then Jeremiah 17 comes into play. You can quote that verse I am referring to. It's interesting that your Bible was already in the book of Jeremiah. Jeremiah 17: 7-8:

"Blessed *is* the man who trusts in the Lord,
And whose hope is the Lord.
8 For he shall be like a tree planted by the waters,
Which spreads out its roots by the river,
And will not fear when heat comes;
But its leaf will be green,
And will not be anxious in the year of drought,
Nor will cease from yielding fruit."

We have all sorts of things going on; it's so easy to put your trust in man, to put your trust in yourself, but you really need to trust God. It is the scriptures that should carry you through. It is the promises of God that you should put your faith in. You should be able to stand strong on the promises of God.

Many people look at Peter and how he stepped off the boat and then looked at the waves and sunk. But every time you don't trust Scripture, you think of the waves of life. Every time you don't trust what scripture says and what the promises of the Bible say, you sink in the water. So, Peter may have sunk once, but most Christians may have sunk tens of thousands of times. They don't trust scripture, the Word of God, over their situation. And in doing so, they are looking at the circumstances and listening to the waves.

There is a wider scope to Peter sinking in in the boat. Peter went on Jesus' word; Jesus said *"come"*, and Peter walked on water on that word "come." He walked on water, and then he looked at his circumstances and sunk. And when the Word of God says, "don't be anxious", "give to God," "don't fear, don't be anxious," "give every request to the Lord," and all those sorts of promises, you can either trust the promises or trust yourself. If you trust yourself, you're not headed for great things.

I want you to know that the scripture works, and as we move into more tumultuous times, as the world goes into judgment, it'll be needed more and more for the Christians of this world to be shining the light and being the light of Christ. They need to be a reflection of Jesus - like how the moon reflects the sun's rays, Christians should be like a moon reflecting the rays of the Son, Jesus. If you do less than that, and depend on yourself, I will see you sink into the waters. We'll see you fade away and see you have trouble.

Recently Matthew switched the TV series that he was watching on DVD. He wanted some variety and so he got out another series to switch his focus. This is partly why different ministries rise upon the earth, and why different denominations exist, and different theologies exist. They all exist to give variety in order to capture a bigger net of fish.

If every denomination had the same theology, it wouldn't catch the same amount of fish. You may look at denominations and different theologies and different ways of thinking as a negative, but have you ever looked at it as a positive that the different denominations catch a bigger catch or fish? Not many Catholics would go to the Pentecostal church, and not a lot of Pentecostals would go to Catholic churches. But within the mix, we catch more followers.

We are pleased that you're taking your time, you're not stressing, but just relaxing during this time. Like I was saying, God's going to bring different varieties of people to this earth. He's going to raise up different varieties of people to influence different people. Some people will know and really love the new people that have risen up; some people will love the old guard, but there's a new guard coming forth. In these days, these people will be practical and demonstrate Christ and not just have ministries that write your emails and say give me money. I'm very encouraged by the life that Matthew is living and hope that you're encouraged by this question.

[Conversations with the Holy Spirit Part 8]

This is 'Conversations with the Holy Spirit' Part 8. I had a friend Dory, who's the sister of my friend Dundy. She had a serious quite time with the Lord, and he downloaded all this information about stuff and blockages and tracks and trapdoors and devices, and things that are satanic and witchcraft that have got into me. It's a very important and a lot of information, and I certainly can't go forward into my best destiny until it's fixed. I was so surprised by the information, and I had a couple of nights with bad dreams and stuff because of it.

I talked to my mother about it, and another friend in the spiritual realm has talked about it. I want to get some insight from the Holy Spirit about that and the timing, and what will go on there. So, this is my first question for the Holy Spirit:

Question 9: Tell me about those complex problems that I have.

Recorded on May 18th, 2020

You' have been waiting all your life to hear what is specifically wrong with you. You have often had counselors who needed you to tell them what you feel is wrong, and this has been disconcerting to you. Now you've got a list and Dory will be able to meditate and expand that list and get something comprehensive.

You have got friends like *Praying Medic* who know some very specific, comprehensive and talented counselors. You should be able to get it fixed. Having the list is quite liberating; I've noticed in your personality and your attitude that knowing is like being set free already. Knowing that specific problem, that normal people don't have it, and that it's been specifically engineered and programmed to keep you back, has provided you with some level of comfort that at least an expert might be able to fix you.

You've been programmed like they program people in the CIA. You've been specifically programmed by some advanced forms of witchcraft and other mind control. So that's interesting for you to know. Dory's information is good, isn't it? It will be helpful for you going forward.

Your mother spoke of three parts to your life. Part 1 was when you did your 55 books. Part 2 was when you entered into a life of rest; and then Part 3 when you become a popular household name.

Heaven wants you to enter into this, what Dundy calls time for intermission. Films used to have one film and then an intermission before another film. You are in this intermission stage, and we want you to relax. We want you healed, at peace and ministering out of rest.

It is going to be a time of refreshing and watering your soul and watering yourself - like Jesus said in John that the Holy Spirit has watered you and washed you. You certainly could do with some washing by the Holy Spirit of God, and by the Word of God. You could certainly know more about the Word of God, so as you preach you could have a bit of revelation. What we want you to do is just to relax and take some time, and just trust that we're going to bring the finances for you to do what you need to do. Just relax and be patient and happy.

The other person on earth that's been talking to you has described this intermission and what you're going to do. So, your mother's real, and we use her, and she loves to talk to you. She loves to communicate to you. It's really helpful.

This week, you've been watching David Servant and the twenty-one-video series on the Sermon on the Mount, and you have been really enjoying a solid Bible teacher. People reading can look under David Servant and look under his video teaching on the Sermon on the Mount called *"A Deeper Look."*

Your mother from heaven has been watching that series and she's been blown away and surprised by David Servant's theology because it's totally opposite to hyper-grace that your mother was involved in. when she was alive on earth. I can see just how amazed you are and how you are surprised at how close your theology was to his, and you're getting so many confirmations of what you feel - and that's really a wonderful thing.

We're pleased that you're coming along with a new project. I just want to give a shout out to Shayne, Dundy, and Mary - and all the people that watch what Matthew uploads on YouTube. I just want to give you a shout-out today. Thank-you for waxing strong in Matthew's life and encouraging Matthew. We love you here in heaven, and we enjoy you. I thank you for encouraging Matthew and supporting him financially, and with your love and with your conversations in which he comments. We love you.

I want to thank the other people who watch Matthew's videos regularly. There are about 50 people who watch these conversations with the Holy Spirit. I want to give you regular viewer's hello and thank you. I thank you for tuning in and listening; I love you guys, and I can minister to you and lead you too.

Question 10

Holy Spirit, are you are you going to give me inspiration for a couple of videos per week so that I can put onto Google Play as an audiobook

Yes, we're going to give you inspiration each week, Matthew. We're going to give you enough things to be inspired by; we're going to help you do a couple of teachings a week. We're going to give you the inspiration and the Bible verses, and the backing and the testimony to be used in your videos to make the audiobooks wonderful. One day you will have a following that's bringing a great income for you.

Right now, we just want you to relax, for the last part of six years you've been really working hard. For three and a half years you put out a new book a month. We just want you to relax with the money, relax from the stress, and relax from editing. We just want you to take some time in adjusting; get ready to be healed and we're going to do an inner work with you. When we allow you to relax, we will do a work that will make you a better servant, and a better steward of the Lord's wisdom.

The Lord is going to better equip you for the future. Of course, we're going to give you one or two messages a week to share, and we can walk by your side. We're going to really encourage you. It's certainly going to help encourage your friends too. A special shout-out to those aforementioned friends of Matthew - you will be special to us, and we really want you to know that.

[Conversations with the Holy Spirit Part 9]

Question 11

Why do you make things so hard in life?

Conversation recorded May 18th, 2020

Matthew, we make things so hard in life so that you can learn and have character, and have personality, gifts and abilities.

Matthew speaks:

I just updated my computer. It wanted to update itself; it's a brand-new computer, but it still wanted to update itself. I let it go, and then it went for about 35 minutes and then finally had a sign-in screen, and I thought that was the Apple ID password. I put that in, and I put my old Apple ID password in and the new one, and then finally I remember it asked me for a login when I was setting the computer up. So, I put that one in, and the computer worked.

I thought I was going to have to take it back to Apple, a brand-new computer. That is the sort of thing I asked the Holy Spirit about; I thought, why what does he allow such hassles?

Why the hassle, Holy Spirit?

A sculpture doesn't happen unless there's been someone carving it. Even rock formations are carved by the river. You know that a sculpture looks beautiful, but it needs raw material and a carver; and we take pleasure carving your life, making you into who you are, Matthew.

We take pleasure; we enjoy carving your life and making you into the beautiful person that you are. You are beautiful, and we enjoy making you who you are. You are a collection of the natural, of the Holy Spirit-imbued part of you, and other changes, psychological changes that you've come to through the course of your life. We enjoy making you into a vessel of clay and have me in you manifesting the character of God.

Matthew speaks:

I've stayed up all night, and I slept at six o'clock and got up at ten o'clock, and did some shopping and some stuff - and went back to bed at one o'clock and slept to nine o'clock. I am in a funny transition again, being a bit of a night owl and sleeping during the day. Of course, my psychiatrist wouldn't like that because she wants me out in the sun.

Question 12

What do you say, Holy Spirit, to my weird sleeping hours?

We have you up during American people hours, and this allows you to speak to Americans, your friends, which is a good thing. You posted your first interview with me with your new video background and three friends (Dundy, Auty, and Shayne) commented on how good it looks.

You've got your angel shirt on again, your angel hoodie on again. Things are going well for you. You are constantly having your patience tested with this new computer and with life. You are a little stressed-out at times, and we just have to mold you and make you into a fine-natured and Christ-endowed masterpiece.

We see that you're taking your medication each day, which is a good thing, and you want to keep mentally focused, agile and in the right space of mind.

We don't want delusions to take over you, and we don't want you to be deceived by familiar spirits or anything like that. We've got you, right? We've got you, and we're holding you, and we're happy with you. You have been through some shocks of delusions, and for about six months you've slipped into a deluded state every two weeks, and you sort of don't want to go down that path, and we can understand that. We can understand that they were traumatic on you, and you don't want that to repeat itself.

We're happy with you, and once again we allowed trouble to carve your character, to give you a better, well-rounded character. We don't have joy in giving you trials and struggles and upsets; we don't sit in heaven and go *'Ha-ha, he's having another trial again.'* We allow them to form your resilient makeup. Life is full of ups and downs to help people determine their character and who they are under stress. It's who you are under stress that really determines who you are.

I hope that you enjoy your night; whether you can go to sleep earlier not will be determined by you I'd imagine. But just understand that we love you, and we've got your future in mind.

We've got your understanding, you're learning, your path, all aligned for you. There are some programs by David Servant that you're watching, on the Sermon on the Mount, or some other things to watch. You can make another coffee, and you can watch some of that; we're happy with your progress today, and you can upload this.

[Conversations with the Holy Spirit Part 10]

Hello, good morning to you; it's 5.40 a.m. for me. This is 'Conversations with the Holy Spirit' Part 10. Today, I didn't have a lot of questions for the Holy Spirit, but I think I'll just let the Holy Spirit speak. He wants to say some things; I'll just let him speak. This is on the subject of free will.

Subject 13: Why do we find it so hard to let the Holy Spirit have his way and speak to us?

Recorded on May 21ˢᵗ, 2020

Holy Spirit:

People find in their natural flesh that they're resistant to things of the Holy Spirit, to things of God. Paul spoke about this resistance in his epistles, Matthew.

He said that the wisdom of God is foolishness to men, and the carnal mind cannot receive the wisdom of God. The wisdom of God flows through my Holy Spirit. Therefore, acting according to the leading of the Holy Spirit can seem difficult, and will for the most part seem counter to what's natural for your flesh.

Many times, I'll inspire you; I'll put the thought in your intuition to do a certain thing, and your mind will reject that thought. You can be sure, however, even though your mind resists the leading initially, if we give you the leading or the thought we will always supply you with the grace to obey us.

People don't understand that our ways are best. People have no understanding that the ways of God are the best ways for them. The world has so corrupted human thought, and so many people are base and selfish, that the ways of love and compassion seem silly, weak and stupid to many.

Many have no comprehension of grace. The plan directed by us, the thoughts, the ideas, the concerns, directions that we have for individuals are the best plans and directions that they should take. Because people have no inclination toward love and grace naturally, they act contrary and people act opposite to what we desire. This is where friction and calamity and all sorts of things come in. The world, and even the church, doesn't think that we're right and our ways that are laid down in the Gospels and the New Testament are right and wise; and they think they are, in their own flesh, wiser. People think that they have a better understanding of life, of its ebbs and flows and what is good and right most of the time.

People think that they understand life and life situations better than us. They think that they're acting in their best interest and according to the best wisdom that there is. When we suggest or lead a person intuitively or inspirationally or with a thought, they can many times reject it and ignore it. When we lead a person to act contrary to what they're acting, many times they refuse to listen. Sometimes we get into an internal argument simply because they don't think we know best. Sadly, people don't think we care for them and their happiness as much as they do.

We always have the best suggestion for people and the best outcome for them. People assume that the commandments of Jesus are wrong, are stupid, are silly. The idea of forgiving the person at your workplace for saying what they did and approaching them and trying to restore relationship is not what naturally comes to mind. They wrongly assume that gossiping and telling their work mates the bad thing their colleague did is more worthwhile and a better way to deal with things.

That's the way people act; they go and turn the whole lunch crowd against their colleague and hope that the colleague understands the passive aggression and curbs his ways. They assume that that's the best course of direction, rather than going to the offender and asking for them to say sorry and forgiving them, like the Bible instructs them to do. They think that spreading gossip, spreading rumors, is better. If you look through the commandments of Jesus, all the commandments of Jesus, the fifty commandments of Jesus, there will be a counter theme that the flesh finds unnatural.

If someone asks you to help them move to a new house on the weekend, it's natural to make excuses and say that you can't. When someone comes against you and wants something from you, it's natural for you to fight for yourself and try and have your way, and not have their way. Just because it comes natural does not mean it is aligned with the law of love and what Jesus taught. What we see that are natural tendencies that a person has are often in opposition to what we want in a person's life. And like anything, it requires practice to walk in the Spirit and to be directed by Us each day.

You don't build big muscles by never going to a gym. You have to continually lift harder and harder weights and do more and more exercises to build muscle. Just as you don't become obese without eating. You have to practice something to become better at something, not that obese is a better thing. You have to practice following the leading of the Holy Spirit to become good at it.

The longer and the more consistently you obey my voice, the faster you become like Jesus and a good representation to the people of God. I hope that you learned from this session.

[Conversations with the Holy Spirit Part 11]

Conversation recorded May 25, 2020

This is 'Conversations with the Holy Spirit' Part 11. I got a prophecy off someone, and I want to discuss that briefly with the Holy Spirit. I have published a book called *Prophetic Evangelism Made Simple.* In that book, it encourages people to do a short prophecy over me. I pray for the people to receive the gift of prophecy, then I ask them to do a short practice prophecy over me to practice their new gift.

This woman had moved into gift of prophecy before reading my book, but when she sought the Lord Jesus for a prophecy for me, she said this. She wrote, 'When I connected the Holy Spirit within my heart, and I asked Jesus for a message for you, the message I received was "Thank you for loving me, thank you, thank you."' So, I sense that message for me was from Jesus.

Question 14: Can you share more of what that message from Jesus meant?

Holy Spirit speaks.

Matthew, you sort of sense this already, but Jesus has a lot of selfishness when it comes to people's relationship with him. He is very emotional about his close friends and makes a lot of effort to keep them close to him. When a person is very close to him, Jesus likes it to stay that way and often times the person does not form many other friendships in life.

A lot of people come to Jesus not because they love him, but because of what they want from him. However, you have such a pure love for Jesus. You have no agenda with your love. You love him like a friend; you never ask things from him; you never want things from him.

You've pursued him so much and obeyed him so much, you've become like him, and you've become a demonstration of Jesus on the earth; so much so that when you go out in the suburbs to shop, you don't have an agenda with people when you're a witness.

You don't try and lead people in a sinner's prayer; you just have just no agenda. You simply go about and love strangers just how Jesus loves them. You have this no agenda with Jesus, you have no motives of your own, you want nothing from him, and he really wanted to thank you. That is why he said to you, "Thank you for loving me, thank you, thank you."

One way to love Jesus is to love other people, and the demonstration of your love for other people is the real measure of how much you love Jesus. You are just infused with the love of Jesus, and Jesus is so thankful. He's quite emotional right now; he wishes he could bestow the full magnitude of his love for you.

If Jesus gave to you the full force of his love for you, you probably would collapse, and you couldn't get off the floor for a week. Heidi Baker went to the Toronto blessing and was on the floor for a week. That's the same thing that would happen to you if Jesus just poured out his love for you. We really appreciate you. You've come on a new journey of discovery when it comes to me, getting to know me. But you've known Jesus for years, and he's really thankful for your friendship. I'm thankful that you asked me about what he said to you. I'm little known to you compared to Jesus.

But you are really are coming to know me through the years as I started directing you. As I take control of your life you are coming to know me better and better. I'm really glad you started with that question.

You have some questions prepared today, so we'll go through the questions one by one.

Question 15: Why do you pick me for this book?

Why is a musician a musician? Why is an artist, an artist? Why is a ballerina a ballerina? Everyone on this earth has special talent; they have been endowed with special gifts, and you've got a gift of connection.

You are like a radio receiver; you can just receive messages from the supernatural. We chose you because you're willing to do it. You're open, you've got an ability to hear, and you like to record these messages and bless your friends. They get blessed by these messages, and they give you feedback - and you enjoy bringing these messages for your friends. You also enjoy hearing what I have to say, and listening to what I have to say, because of your love for God and Jesus, and you've got a love for me.

I love to communicate through a pure vessel, a vessel that's been cleaned, a vessel that's wholesome. I get a lot out of speaking through you. I actually enjoy myself bringing my voice in such a way that can be understood plainly. It just makes it relatable; here is God on earth speaking to people. There are many reasons why I've chosen you, and one day you may go through the effort of making this into a book, and people will be able to read it.

Note by Matthew July 4th, 2020

You can see by the above statement that even into message 10, I still had not decided to make a book. The reason for the conversations were personal and intimate and were for me, the Holy Spirit and my few friends online. The decision to make a book eventually came, but first of all this was to further my relationship with the Holy Spirit, as a journal.

Holy Spirit continues:

People will find that if they liked your *Conversations with God* books that they would probably enjoy these *Intimate Conversations with the Holy Spirit.*

Listen, do you think you are well understood? Personally, I'm not well understood, Matthew. People really don't understand Jesus, and I'm sort of second to Jesus, and I'm not really well understood. There are not a lot of references that people know in the Bible of me, and there are very few experts. Benny Hinn wrote a popular book *Good Morning, Holy Spirit,* and that awakened people's eyes. But there's not a lot of material around about me, and people don't seek me out.

People use my gifts and use the gift of tongues and use healing gifts and prophetic gifts. They use me, they use my power, they use my abilities, my giftings, but there isn't a lot that have a serious, great relationship with me. They call me forth into meetings, and they call for my presence and my glory to come forward in meetings. But as for actually knowing me, having an intimate relationship with me, not many people really understand me.

Not many people really know me. I'm not really well understood. Some people think because I'm the third part of the Trinity that I'm the least powerful, and I'm the least respected, and they feel that I have the least authority. These same people don't understand that I run heaven, and everyone in heaven is led by me, and in a perfect world every person on earth would be led by me.

As we wake you up at twenty-to-five this morning, your brother's staying at your apartment and you couldn't sleep, and I'll let you out here to do this. I just wanted to give people an update; I wanted to speak to you. I really love the way that you love God, and you love Jesus, and you love me - and I really love, especially love, the way that you love ordinary people.

I know that you would love to travel and teach people how to be more like Jesus. I know that you would love to teach people how to be more like you; you would love to do that. You can understand Paul when he said *Imitate me, as I imitate Christ* now.

You have desired to travel and preach for so long, it's like you've desired a wife so long it's become hope long deferred that makes the heart sick, as scripture says. Now, it has become something that you don't strive for anymore because you've just waited so long for it that you've just given up thinking about it. I want you to know that you would be a wonderful teacher to people. I am thankful that you asked this question. I'm not really well understood by many people. I have emotions, I'm emotional - and being God and pure God I've got pure emotions.

It breaks my heart that people use my giftings and end up in hell. It breaks my heart that people don't take the time to really get to know me; they just use my gifts and use my power. It breaks my heart that people don't want to know me. I'm really happy that you're doing this series.

Question 16: Do people not seek you out, or is it a matter of not knowing how?

It's more a matter of them not knowing how to seek me out. You could probably say that less than 2% of Christians would have a conversation with me like this.

It's not really a lot of people who don't want to, it's just that they don't know how; they wouldn't know how. They don't know how to hear my voice; they don't know how to hear the voice of Jesus. They have no concept or no understanding of how they would hear my voice. It's not as though they don't ever think about it, it is just that they don't ever pursue it. It's more because that they don't know how. You've got a book on how to hear from God; that would be a good bonus book to include with this book.

The fact that people don't know how to connect with me doesn't take away from my sadness; it doesn't remove the fact that I get sad that people don't know me. I understand because people have no idea, and it's really amazing to me that so many pastors in churches don't teach people how to hear from Jesus, how to hear from God, and how to hear from the Holy Spirit. You can pretty much assume that they're not teachers; they don't know how to teach.

You can pretty safely assume that they don't hear from me either. They don't think that that's anything important. Of course, if the congregation learned how to hear from Jesus and from me, they might not need the pastor, and that's a concern for pastors. If they taught the congregation how to seek God and how to be directed by God and influenced by God and taught by God, they might not be needed. They are happy being the shepherd of the sheep and perhaps they don't want competition from Jesus or me.

They might not want the Good Shepherd or the Holy Spirit taking control of the sheep. If the sheep were able to hear from us, they may leave. Sadly, a lot of pastors are pretty against allowing their congregation to learn how to hear from the Holy Spirit. That's a sad subject, that's a sad thing to think about and contemplate. But that's the reality of many pastors; they just don't want their people educated on how to hear from the Holy Spirit.

So, do people choose not to seek me out, or is it a matter of not knowing how? It's more of a matter of not knowing how. People aren't educated or taught how to hear from me, and so they don't do it, and they don't know it's possible. What you're doing in this series of interviews, it will be just amazing for some people.

Your friend Dundy has learned to journal and hears from God, and that's amazing. But there are not many people journaling and hearing from God. There is a high percentage of people that can't really hear from God. The Christian Church is largely just religious, just full of religious practices and ideals.

There is very little Christ within us in the Christian Church.

Question 17: Do you enjoy speaking through me?

Yes. I really have a great fascination in getting you up and getting you organized and getting you to start a Zoom video to record what I have to say. Every time you've come to record a conversation with me, you've been fresh, you've been ready. It hasn't been like a chore for you; it's not something that you have to produce every day.

Because of that, I've been able to bring a fresh message and a relevant message. To be honest, I really would like to speak through everyone. I really would like to take control of people's mouths and thoughts and spread the name of Jesus, and spread the love of Jesus, through the whole world. What you're doing here is rare, and what you're doing here is pretty unique. And yet this should be able to be done by every Christian, even not just Pentecostal Christians.

Everyone should be able to hear the voice of Jesus and hear my voice. It's a shame that a lot of Christianity doesn't believe God even speaks today. That's a terrible thing. I really enjoy getting you to a place where you choose to sit down and do an episode. I really enjoy speaking through you and for you to hear what I have to say. I really enjoy fellowshipping with you and you being conscious of me and me and being with you. It is enjoyable speaking through you and communicating a message to you, and through you to other people. It's a great joy for me; I'm really enjoying myself.

If you watch this video and you can see that I've got Matthew smiling, it's really me smiling. The world has bad news going on, and if people only knew me, if people could only see me and hear me, there's a different tune going on in heaven. There's a different tune that I have for individuals. I really enjoy speaking through you, Matthew.

Question 18: Do you enjoy having a voice?

Yes. It's really amazing to have technology where you can just sit down and do a video or have these messages typed up and made into a book. It's a joy of my heart to speak to people and influence people through YouTube and through an eventual book. It's hard being God and not being able to speak to the people that you love.

It's hard being the Spirit with the answer, and yet the people who need the answer are not coming to you. It's hard to watch Christian ministries making choices and making decisions and saying things without consulting you as God. It's hard to watch Christian ministries do professional advertising, and not be speaking on behalf of us, but using traditional advertising methods to earn money for their ministries.

With that being said, I enjoy just coming along down to a simple person and having a voice and speaking forth the things that I want to say, and things I want to say to you, Matthew. I like to say things I want to say to the listeners and the people who read the eventual book. I really do want to have a voice in the world; I really do want some control. You can imagine that the whole of heaven obeys what I say, and yet so few Christians do on earth. Sadly, the Christian Church is made up of a lot hypocrisy, and it can be very religious.

Even grace-filled churches and Spirit-filled churches, all the so-called Spirit-led churches are so full of religion, and they're not always led by me. It's a sad thing. I'm very happy to speak through you, even though you've only got a small number of people listening to the messages. I'm very happy to bring a message and to speak through you in a small way. I am very touched that you spend the time and invest the time to allow me to speak to a few people. I'm very happy with you.

Question 19: Do you wish more people knew you like me?

You're going to make me emotional. I just want to be known; I want to be known in the church. I want to be known by the individual people of the world. I want to be used; I want to come forth. I want to have a voice in the people of the church. You follow a couple of prophets, and you seem to think that they're all about advertising. Their whole message seems to be advertising their ministry, and not so much bringing my voice in my direction. It breaks your heart; imagine how it breaks mine. Imagine how it breaks the heart of the Father and Jesus.

I don't like to be misrepresented to people, and for them to use our voice and our Bible and misrepresent us to earn money for their so-called ministry, because they're supposed to be important and people are going to listen to them. I really do wish more people knew me; I really wish more people were able to commune with me. I wish the average person could communicate with me. Part of the reason for this series is so that people can hear my voice and maybe practice trying to hear me, maybe reach out and start to hear my voice and be able to compare what I'm saying to them to what I said through you. This would be a beneficial reason for this series of conversations. Hopefully, if people start to speak to me, people will be able to discern that it's the same Holy Spirit that's speaking to them when they practice for themselves.

We know that everyone, through their theologies, through their backgrounds, through their influences and through the Bible verses they know, everyone would bring a different feeling to the voice of mine. But it will still be the same Holy Spirit that's speaking through everybody. Thank you so much for doing this interview.

[Conversations with the Holy Spirit Part 12]

Conversation recorded June 15th, 2020

Question 20: Can you lead us all into truth?

Yes, of course, Matthew. This factor is included in the prayers of your friends and your mother and father and the saints in heaven. We factor in your mental illness and the effect that delusional and psychotic thoughts have on you. We factor all that in, and you've become more rounded and more humbled by some of the delusional thoughts that you've had.

It doesn't matter what theology you come from, what doctrine you come from, what church background that you come from, it doesn't matter what stream that you're in, what river you're in, what denomination you're in, we are capable of bringing you to the truth; we're capable of aligning you and your mind and your theology with the truth.

As long as you're open, as long as you're available to be taught, as long as you're pliable and you're humble, we can direct everything to bring you into a place where you're fulfilled and where you're practicing and preaching and speaking the truth. Jesus didn't lie when he said that when he goes that the Holy Spirit will come and bring you to understanding and into everything that he said on earth. There are not a lot of people who really reach a stage where I can teach them the fundamentals and the things that Jesus taught. There are people that I can do that with, but I'm certainly able to direct you to the truth.

I'm certainly able to give you the right books, and give you the right instruction, and speak to you, and influence you, and move through your intuition, and your intellect, and your emotions, to direct you towards what is truth, and what is the right reality, and what is the right doctrine in life. It doesn't matter what doctrine you have; it doesn't matter what belief you have right now; I can correct it. I can do this for everyone reading if you are humble and teachable.

Some people believe in an angry God, a vengeful God, a God where you have to be absolutely holy or you're not going to get into heaven; and you have to be without sin.

Some other people believe in a God that's forgiving, and you can be the worst of sinners, and Jesus loves you, and you can do no wrong, and you don't have to do anything to be holy. They believe that you don't have to obey Jesus, or his commands and they believe that the cross of Jesus finished all the works that have to be done.

Both of those ways of thinking and theologies have errors in them, but there are all sorts of beliefs. There are some people that believe that there is no eternal hell; there is a belief that the book of Revelation has already been fulfilled, and there's no anti-Christ, and there's no rapture. There are all sorts of doctrines and beliefs and understandings that people have. We're able to influence everybody; it doesn't matter what their belief is; it doesn't matter what their dominant belief, or doctrine, or theology, or understanding is. We are capable of correcting anyone that is humble and teachable.

We're able to touch everybody's life and influence everybody's life. We're able to direct people and direct people towards a loving relationship with their friends, with their family, with church members. Jesus, the Father, and I, as well as angels, move across all the streams, across all the denominations, across all the doctrines and all the beliefs and all the understandings - we do our work in everything. We work across everything. We're not so small-minded that we only talk to people who agree with what is right. I hope that was an agreeable answer to your question. Yes, we are more than capable to correct your wrong thought and errors.

Question 21: Do other's prayers help you direct each person?

Yes, they do. It's very important to God to maintain freewill. Freewill is paramount in the kingdom of God. It was through freewill that the angels first fell, and it's through freewill that Adam chose to sin. Freewill is of the greatest importance to God. People's prayers can direct our thoughts, our messages, angelic messages, and direct situations and direct people's lives, but they cannot act contrary to a person's freewill.

Prayers can transform an environment, and lead a person into freely choosing to follow God or freely choosing to change. Prayers are powerful, and when you're praying for a person, be assured that we hear your prayers; and when you're praying for something godly to happen in a person's life, be confident that heaven is hearing your prayers. In some instances, we are acting on your prayers. We can use my Spirit; we can use the angelic; we can use humans, we can use books; we can use YouTube videos, films, TV, radio, songs. We can use all sorts of mediums to challenge and change and direct the person that you're praying for. So, we are big fans of prayer.

Certainly, we would be fans of prayers that align to the will of God, and if you do a careful study of the Word of God you would have a better grasp of what aligns to our will. If you have a good understanding of who God is, and who Jesus is, and who I am, if you have a good understanding of our protocol and our personality and the framing of what is possible in a person's life, you can align yourself to the Word of God, and pray a prayer that is aligned with the will of God and it will be answered.

John 15:7 - "If you abide in Me, and My words abide in you, you will ask what you desire, and it shall be done for you."

If you abide in Jesus, if you live a life obeying Jesus and being directed by Jesus and being directed by My Spirit, if you live an abiding intimate life of Jesus, then your prayers have power.

A personal message to Mary Gibson

I want you to know, Mary Gibson, that your prayers for Matthew are effective and pulling down strongholds and pulling down bondages. You have prayed very effectively for him, and your petitioning, your prayers, are effecting change in his life. So, rest assured, Mary, that you're really loved by the Holy Trinity, and you're really loved by God, my father and Jesus, the Son of God - we really love you.

Holy Spirit continues:

If you're a Christian, you can learn theology, you can learn the Word of God, you can learn what is possible, and you can pray for people, and you can pray for change. You can pray that someone would affect your friend, that someone would influence your friend; that your friend may change his thought patterns, may change his behaviour, and may change the way he thinks.

You can pray that someone would come and influence your friend and change them. You can't pray someone's freewill away; you can't change a person's actions. But you can pray for something to influence those actions so that the person makes a decision to change their bchavior.

Question 22: Are you answering my mother's prayers that she prayed on earth?

This is a personal one, Matthew, for me to answer and this will be helpful for other people. Matthew's mother passed away in August 2019, and now it's June 15th, and so his mother passed away about ten months ago.

Matthew can see that there are changes happening in his life, that his mind is changing, his attitude is changing. He's developing the mind and heart of Jesus Christ, and he's becoming a lot more beautiful person; his behavior is changing, and all sorts of things are changing. He's curious whether we've been using the situation and things so that his mother's prayers have been answered.

His recent admission in the hospital in a psychiatric ward put him on the right medication and freed up his mind and brought him out of a delusional sort of thought. His recent admission that he just came out of hospital a few days ago from diabetic attack has improved his health and given him the ability to function better. Through both admissions, he's been humbled and brought to a place of repentance and change. Through this and other measures, his mother's life, his mother's prayers are being answered.

As he speaks, as he speaks right here, as I speak through him right here, his mother is here, and she's happy to know that her son is being transformed. She knows her son is loved, and she knows that her son is being aligned with the will of God, and the mind of Christ, and the heart of Christ and she's very happy. So yes, your mother's prayers are being answered, Matthew. She's praying more and more prayers as she sees your life and as she sees over and watches your life on earth.

She's praying more prayers and aligning herself with the Spirit of God to champion you and bring you on. For those who are listening to this or reading this book in the future, rest assured that your loved ones, your parents, your people who've passed on, and gone to heaven, are praying for you. The prayers in heaven are aligned with my Spirit and come from my Spirit. You can be sure that your life is being prayed for.

Just like Matthew is being affected by his mother's prayers, you too can be affected by prayers of saints that have passed on. Yes,

Matthew, you really are being affected by your mother's prayers. To be sure, most of what she's prayed for has come to fruition in your life, and she's so happy.

Question 23: Do you direct people in what to pray for in English? I know that you direct me that way.

Yes, Matthew. You have developed an ability to essentially pray in English tongues when you pray. You've learned to be directed by me with your words. You've learned to allow me to essentially prophesy through you, speak through you when you pray. Most of your prayers are fully aligned with my Spirit, and anyone can learn how to do that.

They can just let me place words in their mouth as they pray, and in that way they can learn to pray in tongues, but with understanding. Paul said that he prayed in tongues, and he prayed with understanding, and he loved to pray with understanding. You can be led to pray English prayers, prayers in your own language, and prayers of understanding.

When you understand your own prayer, and you can pray Spirit-led prayers, in your own language, it is a powerful thing.

People really get edified and really get encouraged when Matthew prays for them. When they send a request for prayer to Matthew, and he prays for them, they get lifted up. Most people who hear Matthew pray for them really get encouraged with the words that he says, but he taught himself years ago to pray by the leading of the Holy Spirit. Because he's a prophet, because he's used to speaking prophetic words and being led by the Holy Spirit in what to say in a prophetic word, he is very familiar with speaking led by the Spirit of God; though he maintains anyone can learn to do the same.

Because he's used to being led and directed, and having his mouth filled, by the Spirit of God, by my Spirit, it was easier for him to pray in the Spirit for people, but it's a gift that everyone can exercise. And everyone can learn to pray in the Holy Spirit. It's the best way to pray. You can be sure when I'm leading the prayer, the prayer is going to be answered. So, I encourage you to learn to ask me that I might fill your mouth, and just don't think and just let me pray through you.

Question 24: Do you arrange circumstances to answer prayer?

That's a good question, Matthew. Yes, we do arrange circumstances. Someone who's very prideful may be put in a position that humbles him. Someone who's obstinate and proud may have God Himself come against him. Someone who needs nurturing and needs to be witnessed to may have a Christian join their workforce and become a friend and influence them. Someone who may need to forgive may see a video about forgiveness and be prompted to forgive.

Through my influence and through angels we are always arranging circumstances to change people's lives, to affect answers to prayers for people. We are masters of arranging circumstances to have prayer answered. When you pray for someone, you release the angelic; you release the influence of my Spirit; you release programs and YouTube algorithms and Amazon algorithms; and you release all sorts of miracles to be directed at a person to answer your prayer, to change circumstances, and direct a person the way that you're asking.

Of course, if you ask in the flesh, if you pray in the flesh, if you pray outside of the will of God, your prayer may not be answered. But if you pray according to the leading of the Holy Spirit, if you pray according to the will of God and the purposes of God, if you pray according to the Word of God, then circumstances will be changed, and we'll change circumstances, and we'll change things in a person's life to direct them, to direct a person to the answer to your prayers.

Question 25: Do you speak to people that are not saved?

A simple answer to that is everybody who isn't saved is spoken to by me in order to be saved. Someone is convicted in the Holy Spirit, convicted by my Spirit, to give their lives to Jesus. And so, if I can speak to a person when they're being saved, then I can speak to a person years before they know Us.

Scripture says that Christ died for sinners before the foundation of the world, and scripture says God foreknew those who were going to be saved. With that foreknowledge, there are steps, and there are interactions, and there are plans and circumstances that we place in a person's life to lead them towards salvation.

So, it makes sense that when you're witnessing to a person, when you're sharing Jesus with a person, when you're demonstrating Jesus to a person, it makes sense that my Spirit would speak to the person about you.

They may think to themselves after meeting you, "I should become a Christian. If that's what Christians are like, I wouldn't mind being a Christian."

I can work in a person's life and affect the person and influence the person before they're saved. You can also be sure that the angelic, the person's guardian angel, is constantly leading them towards Jesus and leading them towards salvation, and always encouraging and directing and leading people who aren't saved. You can be sure that everyone who needs to be saved will be saved, and so that was a good question, Matthew. Many people don't know that I work and minister in people's lives who are not Christians.

Question 26: Are you directing us all towards truth? Do we have to be open to it? Open to you?

It's my purpose; one of my chief purposes is to direct people towards truth. I continue to direct people towards the truth found in scriptures. Now people are diverse; truth comes in layers. There's layer after layer of truth. If a person believes in a legalistic sort of doctrine with an angry God, and never measuring up and always striving to be good and holy in God's sight, we've got to give you some information to discredit that and bring you truth and revelation about the saving grace of God. We bring that in a layer, then another layer, and then another layer - and truth is compounded, and truth is laid out step by step, verse by verse and revelation by revelation.

In order to lead a person from error into truth, there may be multiple videos, multiple sermons, multiple movies, and multiple songs that a person needs to hear to develop the truth and come into the truth.

We are constantly moving people towards truth. It's important that you're humble, and it's important that you remain teachable. You need to remain in a position where you accept that you don't know it all, that you don't know everything. You need to be pliable and willing to be taught, willing to be wrong, willing to see error in your own life.

When you remain humble and teachable, then we can direct you towards the truth that we want you to know. I hope this was really encouraging to you.

[Conversations with the Holy Spirit Part 13]

Recorded on June 26th, 2020

Hi, this is Matthew Robert Payne, and this is 'Conversations with the Holy Spirit Part 13." What's a good thing about the number 13 is we've had God and the 12 tribes of Israel - and that made up the number 13. Jesus and his twelve disciples made the number thirteen. Thirteen doesn't have to be a bad number; it was a good number before it was a bad number.

Do you have a plan set in stone for our life? I wonder if I've had an addiction to prostitutes and pornography. Sometimes I wonder when I've hired a prostitute, and I've seen a prostitute; in the course of talking to her, the Lord has ministered to her through me.

Sometimes I wonder could she be affected by what I said if I didn't hire her? I've got these questions about what really is the will of God, or is it like a will of God that God slipped into if we cross his will? It's a question of mine, but I'm interested in what the Holy Spirit says.

Question 27: Is there God's purpose and then a different path? Or is there God's purpose, and we will do God's purpose? And if so, where does the sin comes in? So Holy Spirit, did you get that question?

Matthew, every time you've hired a prostitute, we've been aware that you were going to do it. You know that we're aware that you are going to do it. As for your comment about prophesying or ministering to the prostitute in the time that you're with her, a scripture says that the gifts are not without repentance. In other words, you can use that gift even in a place of sin, even in the act of sin being with an escort and having sex outside of marriage - and you can move in the prophetic gift. My

Spirit can move through you even in the act of sin. People may really throw the hands in the air and say, *"Who is this guy coming and sharing this in a book, like how could he be doing this?"*

Matthew speaks:

I just do it because it's part of my conversation with the Holy Spirit. I just want to be real, and people who've read my books and know I've struggled with an addiction for years. They know I am real, and if you're listening to this and you're wondering what's going on well, this is real. The whole purpose of this book was not to produce a book, but it is first and foremost a journal, and this was a question on my heart. You are reading this as the Holy Spirit encouraged me to make videos and eventually a book from it.

Holy Spirit continues:

God understands the choices that you're going to make when we look at the film of your future. The film shows us all your freewill choices on a screen. I can understand, Matthew, that you really touched that girl spiritually that you saw recently, and you've decided just to see her for coffee now and to go and pay and speak to her again. Was that our design? Was not seeing her more our will? Or is going to pay to see her again for coffee more of our will? That's a question for you, Matthew, answer that one.

Matthew speaks:

I know that her life would have been okay if I never saw her. I know that you've got plenty of ways of touching her, and you don't have to use me. You could use someone else to touch her and minister to her. So, you don't necessarily need me. I feel that maybe the answer is that I finally got on top of seeing an escort, and you would be able to touch her life without my help. I think that's the answer.

Holy Spirit continues:

Matthew, we just want to use you. It is possible for you to contact escorts and see them for coffee, and that's one way you could touch them without sin. But yes, in answer to your question, there are not many people living a truly holy and righteous life; not that it is impossible, and not that we don't love people to do so. But if you talked about a life free of sin, absent of sin, there are a few people who really live that sort of life. You have met a couple of apostles, not self-proclaimed apostles, but apostles that really were apostles and you've seen them live a relatively sin-free life. With the right theology and right healing and right emotional state, it is possible to live on this earth without participating in sin.

What we see in heaven of your future is a compilation of all the choices that you have made. Some are sin choices, some of our will, and you live between those two things. We look at the life that you create each day with your freewill. So, people's lives aren't set in stone; we work with people and arrange events and orchestrate things to line up with their progression along the timeline of their life.

We're constantly changing people's decisions and constantly changing directions, and constantly presenting people with different choices to lead them to where we want them to go. So, it's like a tree going up - branches come off, and then more branches come off, then even more branches come off. A person's life makes decisions like the branches, and we work with people. It's a good question, Matthew, because many people would assume, once you're a Christian, your life has been predetermined and set in motion in a direct way.

People's freewill is important, and so they can make freewill decisions. We know that you've got certain things that have to happen, certain healings, certain things have got to be put in place before the hole in your heart has been fixed. We are willing to work with you to move you toward that healing and we're very happy with you right now.

Your sin does not define you.

There are people who may read this when it becomes a book; there are people who may watch this as a video and use this frank confession of sin as a way to say *"Hey, this guy is a false prophet; he is a false teacher; he's a sinner."*

How I answer those people is "he who is without sin throw the first stone," just like Jesus did 2,000 years ago.

Question 28: Are there many people who fulfill the plans of God for their lives?

That can be looked at in two ways; God has a purpose for each person's life, even non-Christians. Many people make choices that don't allow them to fulfill God's plans for their life.

You like Steve Jobs, who created Apple, and you like Michael Jackson and you even like Elon Musk, who is still living. These are all perfectionists and people with a spirit of excellence, and you've researched their lives a little bit through books on them. Michael Jackson went and did what he was meant to do, and Steve Jobs did what he was meant to do.

Most of their lives were lived not as Christians, although you've seen them in heaven. They were prayed for, and they were saved. They lived their destiny; however, there are a lot of people who never find what their purpose is. They never find what they're here for.

Part of the reason is that this world just takes so much money to survive, and people just choose something and try and survive and maintain their life, but never do what's in their heart to do.

They never make that choice to write those 55 books like you did. They never prepare themselves or put themselves in a position where they can do something that they dream about. People are too busy putting food on the table and paying bills that they never get the time or take the risk of trying to achieve their dreams.

You have written in your book on finding life's purpose, that if a person won 20 million dollars in a lottery and never had to work again, and they could buy a couple of million-dollar houses and have enough money to live for the rest of their life, what would they choose to do? If a person, say your reader, had enough money never to work again in their life and live lavishly, how would they fill your time from that time on?

The answer to that question, if you honestly consider it and answer it for yourself, is pretty much your life purpose - what you would do is pretty much what you're meant to do. It's just the bills, earning a living, and running your family that gets in the way.

Do you know that if you wanted to be a musician and be a recording artist, you can take time to put money aside to record? You don't have to be known by the whole world; your music doesn't have to hit the top of the charts. You can have music that's only listened to by a few hundred people.

Let's have a look at Matthew. Mathew sells fifty-five books on Amazon Kindle each month. Out of fifty-five books, the top-selling book this month has sold 25 copies, and the second top-selling book has sold eighteen; some have sold no copies, some have just sold one. Who among you readers would go through two thousand dollars of expense just to sell one book a month, and that's at 99 cents?

Who would put that effort in - why would you bother? Who among you would spend two thousand dollars producing a book that may never make the initial expense back? Matthew does it for the readers who are ministered to through his books, for the people whose lives improve through what he says, and not so much as a monetary reason. As a teacher and prophet, he has a message to share and for as long as the Lord provides the resources for him to self-publish by donors, he will continue.

That was part of his purpose, and he's achieved a great thing. They are great books; however not everyone will fulfill our destiny and plans. You certainly don't have to be a Christian to fulfill the plans we have for people. There are many people who aren't stigmatized and directed by religion that achieve a whole lot more with their lives.

There are so many opinions that religious Christians have that limit people from actually going and doing what they believe in. Matthew quotes this many times in his books.

A preacher named Andrew Wommack does seminars on fulfilling your life's purpose, and on knowing your life's purpose. Thousands of people go to these seminars to find out their life purpose. When Andrew asks the people who don't know their life's purpose to come forward for prayer at the end of the speech, so that he can pray for them that they'll find out their life's purpose, 80% of the audience comes forward. He has this massive response to his altar call because 80% of Christians aren't aware of what they're here on earth for and what the will of God is.

If most Christians are not aware of God's purpose for their lives, how can they do it? It is just like if you go to a foreign country and are going down a road - unless you see a road sign with the speed limit, you don't know the speed limit.

How can you fulfill your life's purpose when you don't know what your life's purpose is? As a prophet, Matthew helps people work out their life purpose. In heaven, not a lot of people fulfilled what we had planned for them but doesn't mean that they don't have fulfilling lives.

It doesn't mean that they didn't have a good life. If 80 percent of Christians end up in heaven, but not fulfilling what they were born to do, we've still got a good life for them in heaven, and they can certainly start to do what they were destined to do when they get to heaven.

We are not hardcore saying what everybody's got to do what we tell them to do. People have freewill and there are constraints of time, and there are constraints of earning an income, and families and all the expenses. Not everyone is fortunate like Matthew who is on a permanent disability 'living wage income' from his government so he doesn't have to work. He also has to live with the disability of a mental illness, which has caused him a lot of grief and for a long time prevented him from holding down a regular job.

Not every person is that fortunate; a lot of people have to go to work for a living. They can't just stay home like Matthew, sleep when they want to sleep and have a schedule all over the place time-wise and do what we need them to do. Because of this living wage, and because Matthew depends on us, and because of a finance angel that encourages people to sow into his ministry, he has never sent one email asking for money to people.

[Conversations with the Holy Spirit Part 14]

Recorded on June 26th, 2020

Question 29: Do you assist non-Christians? Do you direct them and bring them happiness?

Many people would assume we do not affect the lives of unsaved people and assume wrongly. But they'd assume that God, be it God the Father, Jesus, or me the Holy Spirit, have nothing to do with non-Christians. That's just like saying the sun doesn't come up on non-Christians, or the wind doesn't blow, or the beach isn't full of waves for a non-Christian. How could God divorce himself of his creation? Of course, people hear the Holy Spirit's influence; they hear my influence in songs. They hear the influence in worship; they hear my influence in a young girl talking to her father.

I influence many things that people who don't present and don't confess themselves to be Christian. I am constantly working to lead people to Jesus, as are the people's angels, and people have angels that are constantly on a mission to convert people and bring people closer to Jesus.

It's amazing, Matthew, as you step back up for ten months in doing books, and as you come out of your delusions, and come out of your mental illness and start to get a right mind, you are starting to realize that many Christians have got these blinkers on. You see their narrow-minded ways of thinking; they think that everyone who is not a Christian isn't ministered to by us, and isn't affected by us.

They think that being a non-Christian is a substandard life. The fact remains that people like Steve Jobs and Michael Jackson, people that you admire, had a great life and you understand them so much because you've read their biographies. But Christians, they assume non-Christians don't have the same sort of opportunities, the same sort of happiness, the same sort of joy in their life. They assume that God has nothing to do with non-Christians, and it's as if they're totally reprobate - they're totally divorced from our blessings and our feelings and our love.

The Apostle John said God is love, so how could God divorce himself from being himself if God is love? Surely as love is expressed, God is part of that. Matthew, you may remember one time you were at drug rehabilitation farm, and you were recovering from your wife leaving you. You were talking to a guy who wasn't a Christian, and he was recovering from drug addiction. You were talking about how you're going to miss your son, since you separated from your wife had stopped you seeing your son.

You remember that this guy was able to say that as your son grows older, he'll chase you up. He said that every child will chase up his father. He said just because you can't see him now doesn't mean he won't be in touch. Remember that you felt me - you felt my presence in his words? You felt that I was speaking through him, and I was. I was speaking through this non-Christian guy. You felt the effect that I was having on his words. So many times, I take hold of people's words, and I'm in the creation of songs and love songs and ballets and everything creative. I have a part in so many things.

So yes, I do assist non-Christians, and I do things in their lives because I'm God. I love people, and you don't have to be a cliché Christian for me to love you.

I hope if you're watching this series, I hope if you're reading this book and you don't present as a Christian, you don't identify yourself as a born-again Christian, that you know God loves you. So many people would assume, and that's why you asked the question, Matthew, that we only have an effect on people's lives when they're a Christian. However, you know that we steer people towards ourselves. We steer people towards our love. We steer people towards truth, love, and liberty.

We can take years to steer a person; of course, we can affect a person's life that isn't a Christian. It's important for you to know that, Matthew. It's important for you the listeners and readers to know that we're a lot bigger, and we're a lot more effective than you realize. We're a lot more in control than you realize.

As Matthew records this there are riots and people are destroying statues in June 2020, and it seems like the whole world is out of control.

At this moment, as Matthew hears me say *"We're a lot more in control than you realize,"* Matthew had a doubt as I said it. He was thinking, "Well, how can you be in control because the world's out of control?" Many wars look like they are being lost before their conclusion. I want you to know that even though the world seems totally out of control there is a plan that we have for it. The Bible confirms this. I want to assure you that we know what we are doing and what we are allowing to happen is for mankind to decide who they want to serve.

I just want you to know that I love you, Matthew, and I love you, listeners. I just pray for your friends, if they aren't Christians that their angels would affect them and pray for your friends that I would speak to them, guide them and direct them towards truth.

Even if your friends are Christians, you can pray that I would direct your friends towards truth. Because many Christians need to be liberated from the truth they believe in. We have come to the end of that question.

Question 30: Should we treat everyone as though they are maybe going to be saved one day?

You have this hang-up; it's a Christianese narrow-minded focus hang up that you have, Matthew. It's coming out in your questions, and I'm not angry at you, and I'm not disappointed in you. They are real questions, and they're good questions to be asking me. However, your questions expose your Christian bias. Of course, not everyone has the opportunity to sit down and interview God. Because you have been a Christian all of your life you have a narrow-minded view. Should we treat everyone as though maybe they're going to be saved one day? You should just be Jesus.

Matthew had a dream a couple of nights ago where someone in a dream said 'Just be Jesus.' We're going to have Matthew write a book about it one day. He's written three or four books with sort of that theme, but we may have him write a particular book about it.

People just need to be loved. People out there in the world just need to feel loved, to feel love, and to experience real love and compassion. Believe me; if you are loving and compassionate with people, people will ask you questions. After your love and kindness, they will ask sometimes, *"Why are you being so nice? Why are you being so kind?* This is a world that's based on give and take. People aren't used to people doing them a favor, with no resulting demand on them. They're not used to the levels being unbalanced.

Because you do things for them, and are kind to them and don't want anything back, it leaves them questioning. They are not used to the level being unbalanced, where there's more favor on one side than the other side. People don't like to be anyone's debtor. So, when you're being kind and compassionate and giving, it puts you into question with them. When they question you, that's where you can say, "Jesus compels me to do this, or my faith compels me to have compassion on you. If it's offending you in any way, I'll stop."

That is a whole lot better opening to share the gospel than just preaching it in person: "if you sin, you're going to go to hell." We just want you to 'be Jesus.'

How do you 'be Jesus'? It's easy when you learn what the fifty commands of Jesus are. When you just start to act and obey those fifty commands in your life, your life will change. It's not easy to obey them. If you get the list of fifty commands of Jesus, it's going to be hard for a number of years to respond and behave like that. You will need my help to obey. After a while, however, it becomes habitual, and you start to have the mind of Christ and the heart of Christ.

You will start to feel like Christ, and then when you start to feel like Christ, you can just behave like Jesus to people. That is what we essentially want Christians to do; we want them to draw so close to Jesus that they are like a little Jesus in their community. That is how you are meant to treat non-Christians. Before you have power, before you have the anointing, before you can do prophetic signs and wonders with the gifts of the Holy Spirit you can simply be love to people.

What right have you got to be telling a Muslim that their God isn't God? Who are you to mock the Muslim faith when they are a whole lot more faithful in many circumstances than you? You have to treat them with love and compassion; you have to treat them in an extraordinary way. The way you love a Muslim has to shine and stand out, it has to be different. When you're talking about God, and you talk about a compassionate God and a loving God, and a God that you have two-way conversations with, it will shock them. This is all foreign to them - a God of compassion, a loving God, being able to have two-way conversations with God. They've never heard of having two-way conversations with God. Therefore, the way you deal with people of other faiths has to be something else. It has to be extraordinary; it has to stand out. It has to be more loving than they have ever seen among their own people and faith. It has to be supernatural. For you to make an impact, you can't just make a religious argument with people anymore.

You have to shine; you have to shine with the glory of God. It's important that you understand these things. The typical person witnessing on the street corner is an offense to people. The gospel can be an offense, the offense of the gospel is Jesus died for your sins, and it's offensive to be called the sinner. It is an offense, but that does not excuse Christians to be offensive to people.

I know you're living in a season of being politically correct and not being offensive. I'm not talking about that; I'm just talking about this attitude that Christians have that they're going to tell people they're going to go to hell if they don't repent right now. Many street preachers are bound in religion and their attitudes are offensive and rude and brutal. That is not what we want, and that is not what we endorse. There are so many Christians with that sort of offensive evangelism approach. You will find if you read Matthew's books that he's a lot more different; he's a whole lot more different to other people.

We do want you to treat non-Christians as well as you treat a Christian. Don't assume because they are Muslim or they're an atheist, or they're Hindu, or they're Buddhists, don't assume that their faith is an offense to us. Don't assume that that's a barrier to us touching their lives. Please just understand that you can speak prophetically, or you can heal their sickness, or you can be used in their lives to touch them in a dramatic and holy and miraculous way - no matter what their faith is. Just be an open vessel for us, and minister to people.

Question 31: I've been feeling the heart of Jesus lately, is that rare? Should every Christian strive to attain this?

This is something that you've been experiencing, Matthew, that you've been feeling the heart and the emotion of Jesus. It's the part of you that is sharing that Christians are narrow-minded and blinded, and set in their ways. It's at the heart of Jesus being manifested in you against the religious, the religiosity of Christians, and every Christian is religious; they've all got the mindset, and a vested interest, and a correct pet doctrine and their ideas.

For instance, today you are wondering why you had to share that you slept with a prostitute. You're thinking about that today saying, "Why does it have to be in the book? Why is that in the video? Why do I have to mention that again?" You don't have to mention that, but it just makes you more real. It shows that you're still struggling, and you're still suffering, and you've still got a journey to go on. As we are the people behind you writing and your inspiration, you will already do what we tell you to do. It may not make carnal sense or human sense. But spiritually with our reasoning, which is spiritual, we have better and higher reasonings and purposes than possibly you can understand.

Having that testimony in the book makes it a whole lot more authentic for people to say, *"Well, he's a guy. He's got a relationship with the Godhead; he can speak to each of the Trinity; he can prophesy; he's a great evangelist; he's got a beautiful heart. He seems like a beautiful person, but he's still got this issue that he's dealing with."*

It just makes you more relatable. So, we tell you to do it, and we tell you to share it, and we've got our reasons why we've told you to do so.

So recently, you've been starting to feel the heart of Jesus, and the heart of Jesus can see the hypocrisy and the religiosity of Christians.

Many Christians would hear their testimony of yours, of seeing a prostitute in the last four weeks, and they'll mock you. They'll say, *"This guy is not worthy to teach; he's not worthy to be a prophet; he's not worthy to be leading people in intimacy with Jesus. Look at his sin life."*

You were thinking on the bus today about how many Christians are having sex outside of marriage and how they are not being rebuked or corrected. The church seems to have double standards. Whenever sin is hidden everything is okay, but when sin is out in the open people have issues with it. Of course, we could have made sure that you sin was not mentioned in this book, to make it more palatable for people that cannot handle that honesty and exposure. And yet we know by mentioning it we can not only answer your questions, but also the questions in the hearts of many people who are refreshed about a leader being honest for once about his sin life. We want to reach every person that we can with this book and so we make the choices that we feel are best.

Every person in the world, God dearly wants to bring to heaven, and we just care about everyone. They don't have to be a Christian for us to love them. In your feelings recently you've started to feel the heart of Jesus, and started to feel his mind; you've started to see the religiosity of Christians and the narrow-mindedness of Christians. Through this you've started to get this opinion of this mindset of 'just be Jesus', and don't preach to people - just be this beautiful person.

You are very much aware that the Holy Spirit can talk to a person after you've interacted with them in love and with a smile, and say to them, *"That must be what a Christian is like; that must be what a nice Christian is."* Or their angel could say to them, *"I wonder if that person was a Christian"* and you can plant a seed without even mentioning the name of Jesus.

You are starting to feel this heart, you're starting to get molded, and it's so good - it's a celebration and an answer to your friend's prayers. You have come out of your delusions, and you've come out of your mental illness. You are even starting to come to grips with the John Lennon book not being produced. You're starting to relax, de-stress yourself and stop striving, and there are so many good things going on right now. In answer to your question, not many Christians have the heart of Jesus and have the mind of Christ, and it is rare.

But the second part of the question - should every Christian strive to attain it? Yes, they should. But the way to it is a state of holiness, a state of being that is set apart, and a lifestyle of obeying the commands of Jesus is not a cake walk. It has to be achieved by a determined effort. It's when you're obeying what Jesus taught, when you're acting how Jesus said to live your life - then you start to come into and understand his mind and understand his heart.

When you've done that for a number of years, his heart can start to overtake you, and you can start to be caught up with his mind. It makes a lot of sense to me, the Holy Spirit, and a lot of sense to Jesus for us to have you confess that you were with a prostitute within the last three or four weeks. It makes a lot of sense to us, and it makes a lot of sense to confess that and it stops yourself from being so high and mighty in people's eyes. Many people are endeared by King David, not so much because he was God's boy but because he committed adultery and killed the woman's husband. They may never admit it, but people are encouraged when they hear faults in another person's life.

And for people to be able to say, *"Hey, this guy is so honest - he is really struggling, and he's absolutely free to be able to share this in the book and let that go to print. Yet he's so much like Jesus; he's so full of love and full of compassion, and he's got such a desire to teach and he's so submitted to the Holy Spirit, that he'll just say whatever they say to say. He's so led by them that he trusts him implicitly with his life, and with his testimony."*

Every Christian should strive to be like that; every Christian should strive to have an ability to feel the heart of Jesus and feel the mind of Jesus. That's a goal, and if the world started to fill up with Christians that were acting like Jesus, the world would be saved.

We wouldn't need a last days outpouring; we wouldn't need evangelistic crusades; we wouldn't need what people call a revival - if the Christians in the world were just loving.

Sadly, the world does not know the church by their love. They just know we're Christians by the fighting and their opinions, and every Christian seems to have an opinion. Every Christian, including you Matthew, as evidenced in your questions, seems to be narrow-minded in some way, and they have these vested interests, and vested doctrines, and pet doctrines, and they all seem to have opinions. There is not a lot of love.

We want to lead people through the mind of Jesus, we want to lead people with his heart. We want people acting with his heart and with his mind, and if that happened than that would be a wonderful world.

[Conversations with the Holy Spirit Part 15]

Conversation recorded June 27

Alright, Holy Spirit; this is 'Conversations with God Part 15.' I haven't prepared any questions for this session; I've been up watching a new television series called "The Good Fight." It's a spinoff from the television series "The Good Wife"; I enjoyed that television series and so I'm watching this new series. I'm really enjoying myself. I haven't gone to bed tonight, and so I'm in a good mood.

Seeing that I am in a good mood, I thought I'd do another interview, so that's two for today. I thought I'd start just start an interview with you without any prepared questions and just ad-lib and see how we can go in a conversation without any preparation. I was thinking as I went to get my Pepsi that my friend Dundy enjoyed the question about freewill. And I wanted to explore that a little further because it was a subject that he really enjoyed.

Question 32: Can you speak more about freewill?

Holy Spirit says:

Matthew, you have been struggling over trying to cut the cords and heal your life to a point where you didn't have a problem with pornography, and you didn't have a problem with prostitutes.

You have tried counselor after counselor after counselor trying to fix it. And over many years, you've beaten yourself up so many times. You've tried repentance, you've tried deliverance, you've tried extensive counseling, you've tried courts of heaven, and you've tried everything.

Just even the word counselor upsets you. Your last counselors were doing good, and then they decided to stop counseling you, and they were the best you'd ever found. You've pretty well given up on getting your life counseled; how is that your fault? If you had a choice, you'd be fixed.

So how could it be fair that God is a stickler for everything going right? If Dory, the sister of Dundy saw all these things wrong with your life, how could that be fair? Satan's put all these devices and bombs and tripwires and stuff in your life, with multiple personalities and all sorts of trauma - how would it be fair if you had to get your life right in order to go to heaven when you've tried, and you've tried, and you've tried?

How fair is it for people in addictions and behaviors that they just can't get free of? Many times, they have tried everything, they've tried everything they can, and they just can't get out of it. If the church, if Christians, look at this world through black-and-white lenses and say that you've got to be free of sin and not doing any sin to go to heaven, how fair is that?

I know people have choices, but some of their choices are not their choice. There are forces, and there are addictions, and there are all sorts of things weighing on people.

The idea and the concept of freewill is a big subject. Satan had the freewill choice to rebel. Mankind was given freewill so that they weren't robots. Why is there suffering in the world? Because men have got freewill to do whatever they choose. Of course, there are laws in a society; you're not meant to rape young children; you're not meant to cheat on your taxes; you're not meant to steal someone's property. But there are so many things that you can do and get away with.

It's seems that it is only illegal to molest your daughter if someone finds you doing it, and the world is so corrupted. Sure, there are laws that prevent people from doing certain things, and then there are people that do them anyway. Freewill was so special to God, and yet the whole subject causes you a lot of pain because the world has just suffered so much because of it.

You were looking at a post about three weeks ago by a popular preacher who has influence in Donald Trump's life. The person was decreeing a change of behavior in the Democrats that would be righteous and holy and aligned with God. She was decreeing something that is the freewill choice of the people who vote Democrat to change, and the decree can't change it. You thought that she was foolish, but it's so interesting that you're speaking about this. As a powerful woman of God, she was trying to achieve a change in people's freewill choices and this is impossible, and you were shocked that she did not know this.

What choice have so many people in this world got if you're a Muslim woman who grew up from a young person to your forties, and had a couple of children, and you grew up in the faith. What sort of God would send that Muslim woman to hell when that's all she's ever known? What if she has never met and been influenced by a supernatural Christian? What if she's never met a demonstration of the Holy Spirit's power and seen my power in a Christian?

What if she's never seen love expressed better than in her Muslim faith? Is it fair that Muslim woman goes to hell because she didn't become a Christian? What about a Buddhist that grew up in his country, and all he's ever known is the Buddhist faith and practicing Buddhism? He's never met a Christian who's influenced him; he's never met someone who's had power. He's never met a transformative sort of person, and he continues in his Buddhist faith thinking Christians are narrow-minded people who speak about hell a lot.

What if he didn't give his life to Jesus - is he going to hell? The Christian church have grabbed this line of Jesus to Nicodemus saying 'unless you're born again of water and spirit, you cannot see the kingdom of God' and made a whole religion around the sinner's prayer. People didn't even realize that the kingdom of God was the ability to see the supernatural. The kingdom of God wasn't heaven; the kingdom of God was something that Jesus manifested on earth. They take that one little line and talk about a sinner's prayer, and everyone else in the world goes to hell. Unless you've said that sinner's prayer, you are doomed!

But apparently you can say that sinner's prayer and just go on and be twice the jerk you were before you were saved. Some say that you go to heaven because you said a one-paragraph prayer. So freewill is a big subject, it's the whole book, but you can be sure that it has consequences.

On the one hand, you say that if you go to church on a Sunday and you pray prayers, and you read your Bible, that you go to heaven. Yet on another hand, Buddhists who pray for two hours every morning and are loving to everybody, and chant to a different God go to hell. Because he didn't say your one paragraph in his prayer, and he didn't go to your church, he is condemned to eternity in hell.

There are so many consequences to God's decision, and I know, Matthew, you've been watching; you've been not writing a book every month for ten months now. You haven't been to a church for about eight or nine months too. You can see that the Christian church is just programmed.

For instance, half the Christian church is conservative and believing in no abortion. And yet, if you check the figures of youth in Christian churches, you'll find that a large portion of them are having abortions. Christians are very much against a prophet, or someone who's doing prophecies in ministry like yourself, and very much against one of them seeing a prostitute. But they're pretty lax on fornication, including having a boyfriend that you're having sex with.

There are a lot of young girls, and a lot of young Christian girls, that have sex and have abortions, and the church is so outspoken about how abortion should be stopped, but they don't provide solutions. You've seen it two times on the Internet in 10 years, on Facebook where some ministry was providing support for pregnant young woman. The church is not very good at providing solutions for young women who are pregnant. There are not many centers around who would offer to bring up someone's children until they're ready to accept their child back; not many couples that are adopting and fostering the children of young girls.

Planned Parenthood has provided a solution, and Christians rally against abortion, but they're aborting their children. Every single woman in the churches who's had an abortion is feeling guilty when they're railing against abortion - and would never admit it. She would never come forward in church and tell a Christian friend that she's had three abortions. So, you see, what you see is right - the conservative view that's anti-abortion is wrong on so many levels.

You say a Democrat believes in abortion, and yet a child can ruin a young girl's life completely. The Christian church sadly thinks in black and white; they blame all of the problems in the world on Democrat voters. But they don't realize that the Bushes who were Republican took you into the Iraq War; they don't realize that the Illuminati switch sides and use both sides. Everyone just wants to be right; everyone wants to have their pet doctrine and travel down their own path.

It's the people's love of themselves and the love of money that is an issue; it's the one-world system and the one-world government that are the issues and the backers that are programming society. And you can pick gays, you can pick abortions, you can pick all the gun laws, you can pick anything, and there are two sides to every story. We love the Buddhists, we love the Muslims, we love the Hindus, people of other faiths that aren't tapped into the Trinity of the Christian Godhead. We love them! We love witches, we love homosexuals and lesbians - we love them all.

It seems that Democrats are rejected, witches are rejected, Muslims, Hindus, and Buddhists - everyone's rejected. Everyone but you and your ways and theology. And then you go through all the Christian Church, and if you are Pentecostal then the Baptists are rejected, and Catholics are rejected, and Seventh-day Adventists are rejected. And depending on which denomination you're in, there are all these rejections; everyone's rejected, except people who think like you.

Imagine if God was like that; imagine if we were like that. What if we had a whole lot of rules that you can only have a certain doctrine to get into heaven. Would you know what that doctrine is? What if there was only one doctrine, or a group of doctrines, that you must believe about the Bible that would get you into heaven. If you didn't have exactly the right Christian belief and understanding you would not go to heaven when you die.

What if there was only one, and if you don't fit that you don't go to heaven? Wouldn't you want to know what it is so you could have it? Well, you've reduced the Christian faith down to one paragraph, to one prayer. And you say unless you have that, you can't go to heaven. And yet Jesus had fifty commands. He said five times in John 14 and 15, *"if you love me obey my commands."* And then the Apostle John said that four more times in his letters.

Do you think a one-paragraph sinner's prayer gets you into heaven or doing what Jesus said to do with your Christian life? What do you think qualifies you into heaven? James says very clearly that faith without works is dead. Do you think a faith with no corresponding actions is going to allow you to go to heaven?

It's one thing to say prayers and another thing to be a follower of Jesus. Jesus said, "If anyone wants to come after me, he must first deny himself, take up his cross and follow me." Where is self-denial in the Christian faith? Where is taking up your cross? Where is following Jesus? If you forget denial, you forget taking up your cross, just follow me.

Surely, that would be acting like Jesus, behaving like Jesus, doing what Jesus taught. However, very few, less than two percent of the Christian church are following Jesus. And so, all the other religions are rejected, and only two percent are really doing what Jesus taught. I give that figure because about five percent actually aware that they should endeavor to obey Jesus and the fact that Jesus had fifty commands - and only about half of them are actually doing them.

But we love everyone; we love everyone. Everyone on earth, everyone has put money in a certain place. Everyone has made a decision about money and possessions. According to how important money and possessions are to them, that's how they live their life. A person has to come to a place where they've just surrendered their life. They have to come to a place where their whole life has become a living sacrifice. They have to learn what they're here to do, and they've got to lay down their life and become a living sacrifice for Jesus.

We understand that some lives are tough. Without the mental illness, Matthew, without the sickness, without the rejection, without the hard times, without your wife leaving you and having no friends, you wouldn't be as close to Jesus, myself and the Father as you are now. Without the horrific lonely and persecuted life you've had, you wouldn't be as intimate with us.

Without your ability to hear from me, and hear from Jesus, you wouldn't have written fifty-five books which are a tremendous resource for people who want to learn about the Christian faith. Without hearing from the Holy Spirit, hearing from me to start your Christian ministry and your Christian website doing prophecies for money, you would not have had the money to publish them. If you didn't get over the issue of charging for a prophecy, and if you never started that site, you would have never had fifty-five books.

If you didn't have the intimacy, the books wouldn't be there. Without the boredom, without the lack of friends, without the motivation and the time despair, you wouldn't have 2,000 videos or 850 articles. So, the loneliness and the sadness, and the fact that you want to teach and you want to speak, but no church allowing you to speak, has driven you into this medium of speaking anyway. Therefore, such sad things, such depressing things, have turned out into good things.

Through your suffering, you've become compassionate; through obeying Jesus for years, you've come to have the mind of Christ and the heart of Christ.

No matter who you are, whether you're Pentecostal, or whether you're a person who believes the gifts of the Holy Spirit ceased when the last apostle died, Jesus loves you and wants you to become everything he planned for you to become.

Whether you're a Catholic, whether you're Buddhist, whether you are Muslim - no matter who you are - we love you. You don't have to have the right doctrine to get into heaven. But certainly, if you blatantly disobeyed Jesus all over the place, don't consider yourself going to heaven. Jesus told a parable about the Sheep and the Goats. And the sheep were the ones that fed someone who was hungry. A hungry person is a homeless person. You may have put clothes on someone without clothes, A person without clothes is a homeless person in dirty clothes, that has been in the same clothes for a month. A thirsty person is a homeless person. I was a stranger, and you took me in - that's a homeless person. Most of the people identified in the Sheep and Goats parable can be identified as a homeless person. They can be other people as well.

The parable says, "I was sick in the hospital and you visited me." Matthew had a roommate in hospital, and he was in the hospital for nine days, a couple of weeks ago, because of a diabetes attack. He's been back four times to visit that guy in two weeks, because the guy is just in bed and lonely all day. Last time he was there, before he left, he noticed the guy get tears in his eyes when he said he had to leave.

Matthew speaks:

The parable says, "I was sick; you visited me. I was in prison; you visited me." So many of you listening have freewill; you have a choice to obey Jesus; you have a choice to give. You have a choice to start to obeying Jesus and walk the way Jesus taught. Wouldn't you like to understand what Jesus taught? Wouldn't you like to obey Jesus? Wouldn't you like to start to develop the mind of Christ, and the heart of Christ? Wouldn't you love to meet a person, and have Jesus' heart in you feel his heart for the person?

Wouldn't you like a prophetic gift that you could tell things about the person's life, and tell things about the president's character? Wouldn't you like to have a prophetic gift that you could just speak about an issue the person's dealing with, just supernaturally know what the person is dealing with and speak a solution to them? All these things are possible. Wouldn't you love to understand Jesus' heart for a person and then be able express a message to encourage the person?

Wouldn't you like the mind of Christ to be able to look at the news and decipher the news according to what Christ sees? That's your choice - you can choose to have that manifest, or you can choose not to. You can choose to walk past the next person and ignore him, or you can choose to stop and say hello and give them some money, or buy them a Coke or a hamburger.

Question 33: So how do you suggest we treat people?

The way to treat people is found in the fifty commands of Jesus and found in other suggestions in the epistles. It is in the epistles and all through the Bible. There are so many commands in the Bible. When you have a good understanding of what Jesus and the apostles said, and the Old Testament, and you start to obey, you can start to take every thought captive.

As you get each new thought in your mind that is encouraging you into a course of action, you bring a Bible verse to look at the thought and you judge what you should do. If the Bible verse says do this, you do it. If the Bible verses doesn't agree with what you were thinking about doing, if you take the thought captive to scripture you won't do what you were thinking of doing. If you have a mind that's taking every thought captive, then you start to develop the mind of Christ; you start to act like Christ.

You can say to Matthew: *"Oh, you shouldn't have gone on to an escort site and picked up a prostitute."* I'll tell you something he did do; he went to an escort site and picked the prostitute that his eyes were led to. He is used to picking pictures. Out of six girls, he picked one that he knew that we wanted him to encounter. Let me explain.

Matthew has been doing angel messages for years and typing in in a name that we give to his spirit, like Shannon Jones, into Google Images. Hundreds of images will come up and he is used to picking the one picture that the person's angel looks like. The picture that he chooses will be almost an exact representation of the person's angel. The art of him picking the picture is having his eyes led by my Spirit. He has been doing it for years and years. Many strangers who request an angel message report that the angel picture looks like them when they receive it.

He can type in a word in a photo database and be led by my Spirit to the photo that should be on his book cover. He can pick a picture for one of his book covers, and it will be the picture that heaven wants on his cover. He picked a lot of book covers.

Matthew is very used to scanning groups of photos and picking one that stands out. Both escorts that he's taken out for coffee and developed the relationship with, his eyes actually scanned and picked them. James says that God will never tempt a person or lead them into sin and so you may have difficulty in reconciling what I am saying here. But because we knew Matthew was going to sleep with a prostitute, we led him to pick the woman that we wanted him to minister to.

We were not leading Matthew into sin; however, the gift in him was helping to pick which of the girls that he would have around to his house. It's like someone who's a builder; he could go around to his friend's building site and they could have a house half-constructed. He is not in charge of the site; he's just walking over to see his mate who is a builder and have a couple of beers after knockoff. As he's walking, he can see one of the panels, one of the parts of the construction, that's out of alignment. His gift in him can see it. When he sees his friend, he tells him that the post is out of alignment. The gift in him works in him even when he is not at work. It is not even his construction site, but the gift in him comes out of him. His friend, who is building the house, might say, "Yes, we're going to measure and adjust everything before we put the roof on - don't worry about that. I don't do my alignments until the end."

When you're a fisherman, you know fish. Matthew's father used to come down and visit, and every time Matthew walked past a fish shop, his father would stop and look at all the fish. Because fishermen like to look at fish. Matthew's father could tell how old the fish were. He could tell if they were a day old or longer. He could tell by the eyes and the color of the skin of the fish. Likewise, the gift in Matthew can choose the woman, the one that he is going to have an effect on and the one the we want him to see.

Matthew prophesied to her and even led her in a prayer. She was touched by the prayer and said that she really was blessed by it. That is the first escort that Matthew has ever prayed for in person. She said that she had a Catholic upbringing but has drifted away from that of late and so she was comfortable with a person praying for her.

Matthew, even when he is sinning, is being used by us. Wouldn't it be wonderful if everyone could learn how to prophesy and speak by inspiration of the Holy Spirit, by my inspiration? Wouldn't it be good if everyone could speak on behalf of God? Wouldn't you love that power gift? Wouldn't you love the gift to be able to read people's minds and share with people things that are troubling them, and the solution? What if you combine that with a personality that just loves people? What if you could just be Jesus to people? And what if you had no agenda? What if you didn't say you need to be saved, all you did was just be lovely to people?

What if you just decided today, I'm just going to be a total delight to everyone I meet. Matthew has books called *Influencing your world for Christ* and *13 tips to becoming the light of Christ.* These are two books that talk more about this subject. He has books and resources for you to be able to do this. Wouldn't it be wonderful if you could have power to prophesy, the power to heal, the power to bring a change to people's life?

Matthew speaks:

It would be good if people could be a great witness every day. My friend Dundy was talking about that today. He wished that the church had power; he wished that ordinary people had power to heal and to prophesy.

Holy Spirit:

It takes a lot of work to train people how to prophesy and get competent with that, and Matthew has done that in the past. He taught for years and took a lot out of him, but his book called *Prophetic Evangelism Made Simple* will teach you about prophecy and how to use prophecy to witness to people. The fundamental thing that prevents people from moving in power is the lack of teaching, and also that many people just don't care about other people.

Sadly, many people don't care if people die and go to hell - they really don't care, just as long as they make it to heaven themselves. The sad thing is, based on about ten of the parables of Jesus, not every Christian makes it to heaven.

There is a certain teacher called Kat Kerr who's popular in speaking about things of heaven. She talks about all the happy things in heaven, and heaven is a wonderful place. It's just a shame that half of the people she talks to are not actually going to heaven. It would be good if she actually said how you could be prevented from going to heaven.

For you people listening and reading this book, heaven is a place where Matthew's own father said to him last week that he wished he was in heaven years ago. Matthew's father passed on, and he can speak to his father through the gift of the Holy Spirit, through my gift.

Heaven is a lovely place. Everyone's got a job; everyone is doing something they love. There are no doctors in heaven, and no one needs to be fixed up. For instance, there are no eyeglasses in heaven, and the people don't have to wear eyeglasses as there will there be no imperfections with the eyes. If people are in wheelchairs on earth, they will walk in heaven. There is no sickness in heaven. But there are people that arrive in heaven that are grief-stricken, that have come from an oppressive regime that has bashed or smashed them or starved them to death they take time to adjust. They don't arrive in heaven free of trauma; they still have trauma. These people have to heal in heaven. So, there's a transition that you have to go through in heaven.

I run heaven; the Father, Jesus and everyone act according to my direction. It's like a symphony; heaven is like a symphony being played like an orchestra. It plays according to my direction. So, I not only run heaven, but I'm on earth too.

I enjoy speaking to you guys; I enjoy speaking through Matthew. One day, Matthew hopes his books will be really popular, and there'll be thousands of people reading them. We really enjoy speaking through him, I told him at 11 o'clock last night that he was staying up tonight and he obeys me, and he stayed up.

He is in this 'wax lyrical' mood; he knows that he could have just approached this subject and just spoken ad-lib, and I've used that. I've used the fact that he had been up for more than a day. There are plenty of good things in heaven, but there are plenty of good things on earth for people to enjoy. Matthew enjoys doing what he's born to do, and it'd be really helpful if people did what they were born to do.

It would be really good if people found out what they were born to do and did what they were born to do. It'd be really good if the Christian church came into a place of intimacy with the Holy Spirit and intimacy with Jesus and the Father. Matthew is fairly close to the Father, but not tremendously close like he is to Jesus, and like what he's becoming to me. This is simply because he had issues and trouble with his own father and his father's anger.

He had an argument with his mother about six weeks before his mother died, and when his mother died, his father said that he couldn't come to the funeral. Because of that, he missed his mother's funeral. The hardness and disfunction that Matthew had with his father affects his real relationship with God, the Father.

Similarly, a lot of women, people who've been abused by their father sexually or physically, or men that have had a strained relationship with their father, find it hard to draw close to God; it affects their relationship with God the Father. We will get Matthew into health, have him enter healing again and he'll get closer to the Father.

But I'm the life of this book, and I want to speak it. For those of you who are worried about someone who's sinning and could possibly be so close to us and still have a sin in his life, just thank God that you're forgiven; just thank God that he loves you and pray that a healer may come along and fix Matthew up.

For many years, Matthew called himself Humpty Dumpty. He thought to himself *"All the king's (Jesus') horses and all the king's men couldn't put Humpty Dumpty together again."* And one day a guy who didn't know him wrote to him and prophesied and said, "For years, you've been calling yourself Humpty Dumpty. Stop doing that, I know where your broken parts are, and I'm going to put them back together." And so, he was corrected for calling himself Humpty Dumpty, but he's felt like that all through his life.

There's a certain joy in Matthew's journey; he certainly loves being this close to us as he is. He certainly enjoys what's going on in this book.

Question 34: I seem to mention the fifty commands of Jesus in every book. Is there a reason for this?

Holy Spirit:

The reason is, Matthew, that in the Great Commission, Jesus said to go and make disciples of all nations and disciples in all nations and teach them everything I taught you. The Christian church has got a lot of converts, but very few disciples. How many people do you know personally that are just like Jesus? What percentage of the church has people like Jesus? Is it half your church? Twenty percent, ten percent?

When a church has got a hundred percent of people just like Jesus, then it has been fully discipled. But there's no discipling happening, or very little discipling, happening in churches these days. People call themselves Christians, but they're nothing like Christ. To really be honest, and Matthew has said this many times, a lot more Buddhists are more Christ-like than Jesus' followers. And so, the reason why you teach people the fifty commands of Jesus is so that people would become disciples - and please remember it's us teaching through you, it's not you.

In the parable of the Good Shepherd, it says "I know my sheep, I call my sheep by name, and they follow me." Well, Jesus may be calling you by name, but you're not following, and that's serious. Because Jesus said it, you must deny yourself, take up your cross and follow me if anyone wants to be my disciple. If you're not a disciple of Jesus, where are you going to go? Are you going to go to heaven? It's a serious business guys, it's a serious business. We want you to be Christ; we want you to be Jesus to people. People don't know about Jesus in heaven; they can't talk to a Jesus in heaven.

A lot of people can't operate on your empty faith; they need a touch from God. They need to meet Jesus. They need a human touchstone. Are you going to be that for them? Don't tell him they've got to say a one-paragraph prayer - prove to them your life is better than theirs. Prove to them through your actions, through your words, through your love, through your compassion, through your kindness, through your goodness. Show them that living life like yours is better. Don't preach; don't tell them they have to come to your church. They don't want your religion; they want to meet something authentic.

Don't have an agenda of saving them. Don't make some sort of agreement with yourself like, "Well, if I do this and do this, they're going to become a Christian." Just love people, just love them, just love people. You do your part and trust us to follow people up and show people that that's what a real Christian is like. They might be too embarrassed to become a Christian; they might go to one of their aunties or uncles and say, "Hey, you're a Christian - can you tell me how to become a Christian?" They may become a Christian and move out of your work, and you may never know that you were the reason why they became a Christian.

Christians have got to stop preaching and start living like Jesus. It's so important, guys - it's time. It's time to shine your light; it's really important, it's really time. You can look at the person who's doing this - you can read the words and point out obvious sin in Matthew's life. You can point to what he's mentioned about the escort and say *"Well, look at that! Who is he to be preaching to us?"* Or you can just go and read the 55 books that he's produced and say, "Wow, he's a lot closer to Jesus than me."

We wish you well in your progress, and in your life.

[Conversations with the Holy Spirit Part 16]

Recorded on June 29, 2020

I just pray and invite the Holy Spirit.

Dear Father,

I pray that you would send your Holy Spirit and the Holy Spirit may manifest both in his presence and in his answers and that your name, dear Father, may be glorified, as well as the name of the Holy Spirit. In Jesus' name I ask, amen.

Question 35: What can a little person do to make the earth better?

That is a wonderful question. There are so many people, as you've showed, that you can prophesy to and people can heal and work in the power gifts.

There would be a lot of Christians that are listening to that or reading the book and saying well, "I can't do that, or that's not me. How am I going to have an effect?"

So, this question is for all those little people, for all those people who aren't authors, who don't perform prophecies, who don't work in miracles, who aren't especially called to the five-fold ministry of apostle, prophet, evangelist, pastor or teacher but they're just an ordinary person who sits in a pew each day when they go to church.

Well, like I shared before, you can learn the commandments of Jesus and with the help of the Holy Spirit, with my help, you can learn to obey the commands of Jesus. If you get habitual about that, and you make it a habit to always take thoughts captive and act according to what the commandments of God say, you will become a vessel of our love to the world.

You can become more and more Christ-like, and you will find yourself starting to think and feel like Jesus Christ. So much of how he behaves will have manifested in your life that you start to be become like him. You can make a difference to everybody you encounter. You may not be outgoing like Matthew and start conversations in shopping centers as you walk down the aisles, but you can change the people's lives that you have to interact with.

For example, today with Matthew there was a woman reaching for the highest shelves in the supermarket, and Matthew went to get what he was going to get. He came back, and she was still reaching for the highest shelves. He was able to say, "Can I help you reach for something if there's something you want? She replied, "I'm just trying to find some decaf." And Matthew went and got some decaf that he used to buy. He said, "What about this?" She said, "No, I'm looking for pods. But that's a really good decaf; I've had that before. But I'm looking for pods, thank you." Matthew replied, "Well, it's not hard just to be nice these days. We should reach out and be nicer." And she agreed.

Later on, there was a nice pretty girl that Matthew saw, and he encountered her with something funny about her shopping, and she was laughing her head off with what Matthew had to say. You can just come out of yourself; you can just be beautiful to people. We have this covered before in this series, but I am quite capable of telling a person after you've encountered a person where you have been really sweet, *"That's what a normal Christian is like; that's what a happy Christian is like - like that person."*

I will repeat that, so you understand. Understanding this will take a lot of pressure off you when it comes to witnessing. After you have had a good encounter with a person and made someone happy, or you have made someone smile, or helped someone, I can say into their spirit, *"That's what a good Christian is like."* So that can be the witness.

If you believe me that I can do this, you don't have to announce to everybody that you're a Christian and they can come to your church - you can just simply go about and act like you're Jesus.

There was a thing years ago that said, "What would Jesus do? People wore a bracelet, that had WWJD on it – "What Would Jesus Do? And people wore the bracelet and went around trying to be like Jesus. Well, it's time for that to return; it's time for people to try and consider how Jesus would react in this situation. That's a question you can ask yourself in the middle of the situation, in the middle of an encounter with a person. How would Jesus react in this situation? You know Jesus wouldn't say, nine and a half out of ten times, to a gay person that they needed to stop being gay. He'd love a person. Jesus wouldn't say to a witch nine out of ten times, "Satan isn't the answer." He would just put his arm around that person and love them.

I can even give you the words to say to strangers, and that's mostly how Matthew interacts with strangers. He is given the first words to say to a stranger to start an interaction. He's given words from me. I'll give him words to say to a pretty young female. I'll give him words to say to a grandma, like an older female. I'll give him words to say to a father with a couple of children. I'll give him words to say wherever he is; whatever his encounter is I'll supply him with the words. The words really transform his speech, and he has really good encounters.

These t-shirts that Matthew sells have the glory of the Lord on them. Depending on how many you have, the glory of the Lord comes with them. One of the features of the glory of the Lord is that it makes people more receptive to hearing what you have to say. Years ago, Matthew couldn't keep the attention of strangers very long when he began to chat to them. Now he has 30 T-shirts, and people listen patiently until Matthew finishes what he has to say. Now Matthew has a lot of glory on himself, and people are attentive when he starts to speak to them.

I am not saying to spend a thousand dollars on t-shirts to become good, but that's something you could do. There are so many ways if you choose, if you put down your own will, if you put down your own selfishness, if you take up your cross; there are so many ways if you deny yourself to bless people and encourage them. After all, if anyone wants to follow me, he must first deny himself, take up his cross and follow me.

If you practice self-denial, and you take up your cross, and you put away your flesh, there's just so many ways you can interact with people and make their life better for them. There are just countless ways that you can interact with people, and Matthew has two books as I have mentioned before called *Influencing your world for Christ* and *13 Tips to Becoming the Light of Christ*. Those two books will give you ideas on how to change your life and how to effectively demonstrate Jesus wherever you go. Those two books aren't suggested to sell you things, to make money for Matthew. He makes 30 cents on each book; it is hardly a fortune.

Those books aren't mentioned so that Matthew can make money; they're mentioned as a resource for you. Just like a shopping trolley or a basket are useful to take around a shopping center to put things in, Matthew's books are resources that will help you on your journey and equip you. You wouldn't imagine going to buy 20 things in a shopping center without a basket or without a trolley, and going on in the Christian life and trying to pursue demonstrating Jesus without those two books is the same sort of thing.

Of course, you don't know what's in those books, and you would probably wonder how I could say those things; but I wrote those books. I wrote both books through Matthew, and they're a wonderful resource that could really change people's lives if you took hold of them and put them into practice. So, the message in those books is what you can do as a little person to make the earth better.

Question 36: How can an ordinary person make a difference?

That's flowing on from the first question. Well, first of all, ordinary is a misnomer; ordinary is mysterious. What's ordinary, who's ordinary? There's a saying that normal is just a function on a washing machine! What's normal? What's ordinary? What's regular? An ordinary person would probably be someone who may not be Spirit-filled, maybe just a Christian who believes in Jesus, but hasn't got Bible college education and isn't especially knowledgeable when it comes to the Christian faith. Perhaps they have an average faith; they haven't got a powerful on-fire faith. They may have never met Jesus, haven't met angels, and haven't had supernatural encounters.

Let us say that they are just someone who believes the Bible and believes in Jesus. They don't necessarily hear from Jesus and have not heard Jesus speak. How can an ordinary person like that make a difference?

Well, have you ever walked down the street and seen a homeless person? Have you ever stopped and encountered the homeless person and given them some money? Have you ever asked a homeless person what sort of drink do they want, and go and buy them a drink? Have you ever asked a homeless person what happened to make them be in this position? Well, there's something you could do that would make a difference. Of course, if you said hello to that homeless person every time you passed them, that would build a relationship.

Have you ever been in a church and known a single mother in the church? Have you ever offered to take her shopping to buy some extra groceries for her children? Have you ever offered to take her shopping for clothes for her children? You're an ordinary person; you can tell who a single mother is. You can find out who she is, you can ask her, "Can we make an appointment to go shopping with your children? I want to buy them some clothes."

If you buy a homeless person a drink, or if you take a single mother shopping for clothes for her children, she'll never forget it, and they won't forget it. That's how you can make a difference. I know that many people don't have their eyes open; they walk around this life with eyes that are unaware of needs. Consider the girl serving in the shop when you go shopping for groceries. You can ask her how her day has been, and what does she do for fun when she's not at work. You can ask her how she has fun with her money besides spending it on bills. What treats does she buy herself? There are three questions you can ask her.

You can ask her what she likes to do for fun, and what she's doing on the weekend. The next time you see her, you can ask, "How was your weekend? Did you do such and such?" You can have an ongoing conversation with a person. You can go out of your way to make people who serve you feel special; that's something you can do. You're an ordinary person; you can think of ways to encourage and bless people.

With people that you meet in your day-to-day life, you can ask them what they do for fun; you can ask them what makes them happy; you can ask them about their life. People love to be asked questions about themselves and they love for people to take an interest in them. They especially love it when you seem to remember the last thing they said to you. People are really impressed when you seem to take a real interest in them. They are even more impressed when they *"feel"* that you don't have an agenda of converting them.

You don't need to tell them that they need to give their life to Jesus, or that if they don't get saved that they are going to go to hell. You don't have to preach that normal gospel that Christians seem to preach; you can just bless people, encourage people, and get people in conversation. Be a difference to people; be someone different.

Matthew is extraordinarily good with this. There's no one that he's ever been out with that's more outgoing than himself. His friends know that he'll regularly stop and start talking to a person and engaging a person. His friends are aware of this and are happy that it happens. However, they don't join in and engage a person. Matthew looks forward to having a friend one day who can engage and carry on the conversation with him, with a stranger.

There are so many things an ordinary person can do. Giving money is important, and ministries survive with money, and you can send money to Matthew and support his ministry if you choose. But money's easy - let me clarify this. It's easy to send money, even though money is a hard thing for people to part with.

When you send money you don't have to do anything. Like if you sent money to Heidi Baker, it's Heidi Baker that gets it at six a.m. and prays till 11 a.m. and spends five hours in prayer and then goes off and has to do miracles every day just to survive. It's Heidi Baker that does the hard work; you are sending her a hundred dollars - that's as easy as just withdrawing a hundred dollars out of your bank account. It's not a lot of effort; it's actually more beneficial for you to go out to your shopkeepers, and the people you interact with, and bless everyone and be beautiful to everyone. That is a lot more beneficial. It would be better if you gave a hundred dollars out to homeless people that you meet bit by bit. It would be better if you spent a hundred dollars on the single mother's groceries and buy some treats for her.

I don't want to discourage you from sending money to ministries. But I want you to know that sending money is easy. It's a lot harder becoming like Heidi Baker. Becoming a person who stops for the one in front of you that has a need, a popular message of Heidi, is more beneficial for you to do than to just send her ministry money. She says that ordinary people should just stop for the person in front of them. When the person in front of them has needs, you should stop and address those needs. That's her message - it's a powerful message, but people in the West don't seem to understand the message.

It is not that she isn't a good communicator. She shares it, and people just don't seem to capture it, they don't seem to understand. As an ordinary person, you can make a difference. You know ordinary people need to be saved by ordinary people. There are a lot more ordinary people out there than superstars in the Christian faith, and in anything.

There's a lot of boys that play football, that play soccer. There are millions and millions of boys that play soccer. But there's only a few hundred that play on the world stage. All the boys playing soccer in the streets as they grow up are ordinary children. All the ones that play on the world stage are superstars. The same is true in the church. There are a lot more ordinary people than popular preachers and evangelists. The boy playing soccer in the backyard in Venezuela has more of an effect on his friend as his friend grows up than a superstar.

The friend of the boy playing soccer in the backyard in Venezuela, that friend will never meet a superstar soccer player, but his friend playing soccer with him in the yard can influence him. So, my point is that it's the ordinary people that have to rise up and be powerful. It's not the five-fold ministry, it's not the superstars in ministry that should be called upon to save the world.

It's the ordinary people; it's the people like you that are called. So, get your t-shirts on, buy one of the 200 t-shirts that Matthew has. Find a t-shirt that you'd like to engage on that subject. Go out and ask people if they like your t-shirt and engage people in conversation. Start talking about Jesus, start talking about life, start talking about their life.

Start changing people's lives; start being a difference in people's lives.

Closing thoughts

It was an act of pure obedience to include details of my sin life in this book. It has been 6 weeks since I have slept with an escort and I feel I am having victory in this area as well as pornography. My good friend, Dundy, agrees that my failures should remain in the book as he says it encourages people that they don't have to be perfect to be used by the Lord Jesus. Please pray that I remain free of these sins that have plagues my life for so long.

It is my prayer that you not only learned about the Holy Spirit, and the ways of Jesus, but I hope that it encourages you to seek to learn how to speak to the Holy Spirit yourself and keep your own journal.

Be blessed

Matthew Robert Payne

July 2020

BLURB

The Holy Spirit is alive and waiting to speak to you. For too long the Holy Spirit has been ignored or simply used for His gifts and not even considered as a person of the Trinity that one could have an intimate relationship with. In *Intimate Conversations with the Holy Spirit*, you will find Matthew's journey into getting to know the Holy Spirit.

Come and listen to this private journal as Matthew opens up to the Holy Spirit about his life, his problems and his sins, and listens to the advice and comfort that the Holy Spirit brings to him. Come and listen to how the Holy Spirit wants to be known and loved and what the Holy Spirit wants from us as Christians. If you have never personally been close to the Holy Spirit, let this book be a prequel to your own journey toward speaking to the Holy Spirit in your own journal.

In this book you will find that the Holy Spirit is easy to talk to, is approachable and has a lot of wisdom for the person who wants to approach him. It is hoped through this book and the resources mentioned in this book that you will become more Christ like and able to act and behave like Jesus in your very day encounters from this time on.

FREE BONUS BOOKS

In the Kindle version of this book, which is free if you buy the paperback, you will find two other free books, written by Matthew Robert Payne. They are called *"How to hear God's Voice"* and *"Influencing your life for Christ"*.

I'd Love to Hear from You

One of the ways that you can bless me as a writer is by writing an honest and candid review of my book on Amazon. I always read the reviews of my books, and I would love to hear what you have to say about this one.

Before I buy a book, I read the reviews first. You can make an informed decision about a book when you have read enough honest reviews from readers. One way to help me sell this book and to give me positive feedback is by writing a review for me. It doesn't cost you a thing but helps me and the future readers of this book enormously.

To request your own personal prophecy, or receive a personal message from your angel, or receive a comprehensive destiny prophecy, you can also visit my website at http://personal-prophecy-today.com. All of the funds raised through my ministry website will go toward the books that I write and self-publish.

To write to me about this book or to share any other thoughts, please feel free to contact me at my personal email address at survivors.sanctuary@gmail.com.

You can also friend request me on Facebook at Matthew Robert Payne. Please send me a message if we have no friends in common as a lot of scammers now send me friend requests.

You can also do me a huge favor and share this book on Facebook as a recommended book to read, which will help me and other readers.

How to Sponsor a Book Project

If you have been blessed by this book, you might consider sponsoring a book for me. It normally costs me $1,500—and sometimes more—to produce each book that I write, depending on the length of the book. If you seek the Holy Spirit about financing a book for me, I know that the Lord would be eternally grateful to you.

Consider how much this book has blessed you and then think of hundreds or even thousands of people who would be blessed by a book of mine. As you are probably aware, the vast majority of my e-books cost ninety-nine cents, which proves to you that book writing is indeed a ministry for me and not a money-making venture. I would be very happy if you supported me in this.

If you have any questions for me or if you want to know what projects I am currently working on that your money might finance, you can write to me at survivors.sanctuary@gmail.com and ask me for more information. I would be pleased to give you more details about my projects.

You can sow any amount into my ministry by simply sending me money via the PayPal link at this address: https://personal-prophecy-today.com/support-my-ministry/.

You can be sure that your support, no matter the amount, will be used for the publishing of helpful Christian books for people to read.

Acknowledgments

Dundy, Shayne and Mary

I want to thank my personal friends Dundy, Shayne ad Mary for listening to me from day to day and supporting me. Without a mother and father these days, friends are important and their input is valuable to me as I pursue what the Lord has called me to.

Readers and ministry supporters:

I want to thank the readers of my books and my ministry supporters for the funds that you have given me to publish books. I live to educate people, and I thank my readers and the supporters of my ministry because you make life worth living.

Bill Vincent

I want to thank Bill Vincent from RWG Publishing for getting this book to market for me and all the preparation that it took.

About Matthew Robert Payne

Matthew Robert Payne, a teacher and prophet, enjoys writing what the Lord puts on his heart to share. He receives great pleasure from interacting with others on Facebook, hearing from people who have read his books, and prophesying over people's lives. He is a passionate lover of and disciple of Jesus Christ. He hopes that as you discover his books, you will intimately come to know Jesus, the Father, and Matthew through his transparent writing style.

Matthew grew up in a traditional Baptist church and gave his heart to Jesus Christ at the tender age of eight years old. But he left home at the age of eighteen, living a wild life for many years and engaging in bad habits and addictions. At twenty-seven, he was baptized in water and, at the same time, baptized in the Holy Spirit. Matthew learned about the five-fold ministry offices and received a revelation of their value today.

He started his journey as a prophet twenty years ago, learning about this gift and putting it into practice. With thousands of prophecies under his belt, he can confidently prophesy to friends and strangers alike. He has been writing for a number of years and self-published his first book in 2011. Today he spends his time earning money to self-publish. You can find over two thousand of his videos on YouTube under Matthew Robert Payne.

You can connect with him on Facebook. You can sow into his book-writing ministry, receive a message from your angel, or even receive your own nine-minute personal prophecy from Matthew at http://personal-prophecy-today.com.